Be Not Afraid

Be Not Afraid seeks to give help, to bring
peace of soul and provide compassionate
understanding for those who are afraid.
Perhaps, in their hearts, men have always
been afraid but surely never more so than
now. The unceasing and increasing pres-
sures of our complex society and the mental
chaos brought by the tumbling of values
long accepted as immutable make this a
most timely book. Vanier's words and
thoughts are liberally buttressed with
quotations from the scriptures. Like his
other books this one will mean many things
to many people.

Be Not Afraid

by Jean Vanier

PAULIST PRESS
New York/Ramsey/Toronto

The Scripture quotations in this publication are from the Revised
Standard Version Common Bible, copyright © 1973, by the Division of
Christian Education of the National Council of the Churches of Christ in
the U.S.A. and used by permission.

First published in Canada by Griffin Press Limited, 461 King Street West,
Toronto M5V 1K7, Canada

Published in the United States of America by Paulist Press
Editorial Office: 1865 Broadway, N.Y., N.Y. 10023
Business Office: 545 Island Road, Ramsey, N.J. 07446

ISBN: 0-8091-1885-8

Printed and Bound in Canada

Contents

Preface.............................. vii

1　Two Worlds......................... 1

2　The Kingdom Between............... 21

3　Jesus the Healer.................... 37

4　Grow.............................. 55

5　Become a Shepherd................. 67

6　Share Together.................... 77

7　Love Your Neighbour............... 87

8　Abide in My Love..................105

9　Come Forth........................113

10　Come to the Wedding Feast..........125

11　The Gift of Today..................137

Preface

These pages were first of all spoken. The first two chapters come from talks in Ottawa in 1971, and have been published in French in *Ouvre Mes Bras*.* The rest comes from a retreat which I gave in Winnipeg in 1973.

It has been a deep source of grace for me over these last years to share with men and women who are yearning for love. I thank those who were present at these talks; it is their desire for truth which drew these words from me. I know that I do not live what I preach, however much I desire to do so. At the same time, I am conscious that these are not my words: they are the message of Jesus, even if, alas by my lack of love, I have not been able to give this message in all its force and purity.

His message is eternal and life-giving and corresponds to a deep need in the human heart. My experience at L'Arche over the last ten years and my experience with wounded people — men and women in prison, young people who are confused and lost — convince me more and more that all of us are yearning for love. In our world, with all its false values, we can too often see only egoism, indifference and a search for material things. We all yearn for love and yet it can seem impossible to reach. This is why our world is so sad and why so many people live close to depression, frustration and aggression. This is why so many people throw themselves into hyper-activity, seeking unending pleasure and riches and power. This is why so many people build up barriers and hide behind them. Love seems impossibly distant and people are afraid.

* Paris, Editions Fleurus, 1973

And yet once people sense that love is possible, they awaken and respond to it so quickly. I have always been impressed, in all the retreats, by the fact that it is the wounded and handicapped people, the people with few intellectual abilities, who are especially open to the message of Jesus the Lover. Perhaps they are in some way obliged to seek the essential and the eternal, because they know they can reach few of the goals of this world. Jesus enables them to accept their handicaps and to become sources of life and of love. Their smile and their peace can confound the sadness of those of us who own material things and are taken up by activity.

I have learned more about the Gospels from handicapped people, those on the margins of our society, those who have been crushed and hurt, than I have from the wise and the prudent. Through their own growth and acceptance and surrender, wounded people have taught me that I must learn to accept my weakness and not pretend to be strong and capable. Handicapped people have shown me how handicapped I am, how handicapped we all are. They have reminded me that we are all weak and all called to death and that these are the realities of which we are most afraid. They have shown me how much I need Jesus the Healer. It is only when we accept these things that we can learn to open ourselves to the Spirit of love which Jesus promised us. Jesus came to give life and to give it abundantly. He calls us from death to life, for He, the Lamb of God, took death on Himself and conquered it. He came to preach good news to the poor, liberty to the oppressed and freedom to captives (*cf.* Luke 4, 18). Some of us are captives of our own misery and loneliness, others of false values and possessions; all of us are captives of our fear. Jesus came to free us all by the gifts of His Spirit and calls us to a new life of the Beatitudes and of community.

As I feel more and more the injustice, the inequalities and the exploitations of this world, I understand better why so many people throw themselves into political activity which aims to destroy the power-structure of our society. I understand better why people who are frightened of losing their possessions and power try to defend themselves and the structures which support them. Our world is moving towards universal conflict, pushed by the jealousies and hatred which come from fear. Jesus came to destroy hate and to lead all men into fraternity, universal love and peace. But this means that we must all reject our individual and group egoisms; we must all learn to die to ourselves and, reborn in the Spirit, to live for our brothers and for God our Father. I believe that the world will only change as people's hearts change and as people open themselves to love and tenderness. Our political and economic structures reflect our inner fears; they can only be changed as hearts change. This does not mean that we must not struggle against injustice on a political level, for we must. But above all we must become sources of love for others; we must become attentive to the little people, the wounded, the fragile and the lonely people. It is as this current of life grows stronger that structures will change.

But to help wounded people grow, we must commit ourselves to them and live with them in community. I believe deeply in community, in community inspired by Jesus and His Spirit. It is communities of love which will bring new life and enable people to drop their barriers of fear.

Jesus calls us to love each other and to build community, and He manifests Himself and His love through community. We begin to discover that love is possible through the power of His Spirit and our union with our brothers and sisters. Our yearning for love is met and at the same time grows stronger. Hope is born and we can go forward, walking firmly but humbly towards the wedding feast which is promised for all humanity.

Pray for me, my brothers and sisters, that I may be faithful to this call. Pray that together, by our love, we will all become instruments of peace in this world of ours, this world so wounded by fear.

This book owes a great deal to Deanne Waters, who worked on the texts of the retreats, to Teresa de Bertodano, who helped translate the French, and to Ann Shearer who worked hard to put everything together. My thanks go to them and to all who called me forth, especially to my brothers and sisters of L'Arche.

Jean Vanier
August, 1974

These pages I give

to Mary

the silent one

      compassionate

      and loving

      who is not afraid to

      say "Yes" to Love.

Two Worlds

Everywhere around us
we see two worlds
   The world of misery
   the world of those who wait
   the world of those trying
      to get out
Then the other world
the world of riches
the world of those shut up
in harshness and security

   Between these two worlds
   a huge wall
   which prevents direct contact
   meeting, communion
   sometimes there may be
   exchanges
   but never any direct contact

The comfortable throw money
or things
over the wall
but the last thing
they want
is to see or touch

They send roses
they don't give them
they throw them
over the wall
faded roses
almost dead
but they look like a present

"What does it matter?
They'll make them happy
those others
those poor creatures
on the other side."

It helps us believe
we are superior
and makes others believe
the same
because we are the kind of people
who are able to help
our inferiors

New York is the greatest city in the world
huge avenues
crowds — eight million people
lights
skyscrapers
luxury
smart shops
nightclubs
huge cars
fur coats
hats
big hotels
four-star restaurants
whisky

New York has all the signs of richness and opulence
in the dark streets
lights blotted out by skyscrapers
a man walks
bowed down by loneliness

That great crowd
but he knows no one
the sad faces of people taken up with nothing
running
business men
being busy

                         Then you go into the black area
                                    of Harlem
                         and other neighbourhoods
                         such sadness
                         faces battered
                         faces wounded
                         faces humiliated
                         strangers
                         Puerto Ricans

How is it possible?   so much misery
                         so much suffering
                         so much filth

New York — city of contrasts

power and riches
money jangling
then   everywhere
                       filthy streets
                       poor people
                       tramps

So you say there must be something else
and you search
you search for
someone
true
living
radiant communities
        which give out life
                  joy
                  simplicity
       animated by love
                by the Holy Spirit

Between these two worlds of opulence and misery
some faces of light
with the look of peace
    the smile
that comes from the depths of silence
                    from a love drawn
                    from outside this world

Faces shining
faces lined by tears
at the sight
   the touch of so much misery
             so much injustice
             so much scorn

             so many deaths

I was in New York and I felt ill at ease. I needed to find places and people with the Holy Spirit living in their hearts — a community of peace and love.

In a Greenwich Village house I met a group of thirty women who were coming out of a long spell of drugs and prostitution. They were not beautiful, because the drugs and the prostitution had left their marks on their faces and in the heaviness of their bodies. But I felt at peace. They were simple and open. We talked for at least two hours. I spoke very freely of the problems I sometimes face with handicapped people who can disperse their anguish only through violence. They began to tell me of their difficulties, of the way in which they lived in this house and how they were trying to find another road. I was astonished at the unaffected way in which they gave these confidences — this was real! I thought of so many other people, living in opulence, who do not speak so simply and who are afraid of revealing themselves. They hide behind their riches.

I met a priest there at the same time. He lived in a black parish with 132,000 inhabitants. Twenty thousand, he told me, took heavy drugs like heroin or others which are less harmful — twenty thousand!

4

So you can understand why it is dangerous to walk in New York city at night. Taking heavy drugs means an outlay of ten or twenty dollars a day, and this means having a lot of money. If you haven't got it, but can't do without the drug, you attack passers-by for their money. In the midst of this hell of drugs are these women, trying to get out, helped also by this priest.

There is also Little Brother Joe, an Italian, who works in this sick area. He feels a bit crushed, because it is crushing to live in difficult situations. But Joe laughs. He is marvellous. Sometimes he works in the house of the women who have been on drugs for a long time and he laughs with them. He is very simple. You feel that he is a man alive with the Holy Spirit. He did me good.

He took me to the chapel of the Little Brothers, in the heart of a dirty street, cluttered with people. The chapel was the back room of their shop, a tiny room without a window, but full of a great silence. Looking at the cross above the tabernacle and feeling the weight and the lightness of the silence which flowed into my body, I understood where Little Brother Joe found his strength and his smile.

Later, I met Dorothy Day. She is not very young any more, but she remains a symbol of the kind of person who, practically without means, struggles for justice and truth and does not let herself be crushed by the gigantic mountain of tyranny, despair and luxury. She lives in an area where there had been several murders recently. Her house is always open to the out-of-work, to beggars, to the poor of all kinds. We had a cup of tea in the main room, surrounded by some of these poor people. Dorothy is dressed very poorly, and her face is lined with years of struggle. But her eyes are illuminated by the living love which dwells in her.

Afterwards, I visited other places. We met a group of Pentecostals, full of dynamism. They prayed together, and their prayer meeting was alive with hope, and with the love of Jesus. The Holy Spirit manifests itself at these meetings, perhaps in a rather effervescent way. We must hope that with time the rather exalted and more exterior aspects will be transformed into a stable, compassionate tender presence: Mary at the foot of the Cross, Mary very close to the crucified ones, manifesting her tenderness.

Yes, between these two worlds
of opulence and misery
some faces of light.

When I visit India, I also have, but in a different way, this feeling of being faced with a reality which implies over-whelming and totally insoluble situations. The gap between riches and poverty in India is monstrous. On one side, a crowd of people, a stagnant mass, pressed together, a world of dirt: the sick, the dying — a real leprosy of humanity. And then a woman who arrives in a chauffeur-driven car, who plays golf on a huge course, who is alone with her riches. Calcutta — folly of riches and misery.

I think of the slums of Bombay, in which thousands of people stagnate in squalor and poverty. The population of these slums increases each year by three to five percent through births alone. Thousands of people more each year! How can one even speak of "people" in this immense mass of humanity? Yet, they are people.

Who can call forth hope in the face of the miseries of riches and of poverty?

The eyes of Mother Teresa and her sisters. I met Mother Teresa in Bombay. An extraordinary face, a face full of compassion. She is young. She is hardly sixty, and seems at times eighty. You feel her tired, broken, crushed, but in spite of everything, so young, so open and creative. She has created houses for the dying in India. She has founded, with her Indian sisters, a house in Harlem, in New York, and others in London, in Africa and around the world.

Her sisters in Amman, at the time of the civil war, passed through moments of anguish. Wherever there are hot spots in the world, you find these little sisters giving themselves totally — working, smiling, completely peaceful, always ready to help the rejected, living as poorly as those around them. There is always a big cross in their chapels, and beside the cross the last words of Jesus: "I thirst". And then there are those faces of the Little Sisters of Charles de Foucauld, living in the slums, working in the factories, a ray of hope where there is suffering.

It's important to see people full of the Holy Spirit. They carry a hope. They act. They even sink. But they never say that they are conquered by despair and by the mountain of injustice, indifference, materialism and violence. Often, those who are moved by the Holy Spirit have few means and little money, but their heart is one of hope. Mother Teresa and Little Sr. Madelene of Jesus own nothing. They have only their being, their strength of love, their confidence in the Spirit, a dynamism which comes from a thirst for justice and from a deep union with Jesus. They have also their weaknesses, their limits, their problems, their fatigue. But they do not stop working for the despairing of the world.

Calcutta

Men die   alone in the street
                 or in the arms of sisters
                 full of hope
                 for Jesus has conquered death

Lepers
sick men lost in a miserable mass
leprosarium of humanity

                 What can I do?
                 It's India
                 It's far away
                 It's not my home

It's not my home

7

I reassure myself
I forget

> It's too far
> I can't do anything
> Well — maybe send some clothes or
> money?

But we don't have to go to India. There are so many sad situations close to us. How many more times can we calmly tolerate, forgetting the next moment, the sight of a poor man picking out of the dustbin the fruit or the bread we have thrown out, because it isn't fresh enough for us?

How many more times can we fail to be shaken to the depths of our beings by the woman who shouts in the street and whom everybody rejects: "Leave her, she's mad"?

How long can we go on giving a penny to the beggar without looking at him, because we are afraid of him?

How long can we go on shutting our eyes to, or finding a thousand reasons to justify, the insufferable situations that we meet each day in our homes, in our neighbourhoods, in our towns?

How long can we force ourselves to forget, to justify misery so that we remain free of uncomfortable involvement? How long can we go on accepting the atrocious situations in which so many handicapped people, prisoners and so many wounded ones, find themselves?

How long can we go on perpetuating the universal division between the world of the well-thought-of, the comfortable, and the world of the rejected, of those who suffer and are in distress?

There are all those distressed people we meet every day in the street and don't see any more — or don't want to see — or whom we judge and exclude by the way we look at them; this crowd of miserable people in our towns, whose existence we do not perhaps even suspect. The psychiatric hospitals are full: it is unbearable to go into a room where eighty men, more or less dressed, are left to themselves, without occupation or activity of any kind. And how many desperate people are hidden in our towns, in the apartments right next to us?

Paul arrived in Trosly about twenty days before I left for Canada. He had nothing except what he was wearing — no money, no suitcase. He hated his father who drank, and who was, he said, "no good". He liked his mother, but he hadn't seen her for a long time, because she had remarried and he didn't get on with her husband.

Paul was twenty-six, with psychotic traits in his face, defences against a world which did not accept him. When you find yourself in a world where you meet only people who hate you, a world without understanding or love, you shut yourself away, you retreat into yourself as a defence against being totally destroyed. Paul had been in prison for vagrancy several times. He had also had several spells in psychiatric hospitals before being directed to us by friends. What did he need? He needed someone who would say to him: "I love you and am concerned about you." Of course he would try all sorts of tricks to see if what we said corresponded to what we really thought and tried to live.

Paul had hardly ever worked in his life and had no wish to do so. So I told him that there was no reason why he should, that I couldn't see much point in him trying to work. But I did see a certain future for him as a vagabond, and I telephoned a friend in the south of France, where the weather is better and it is more pleasant to be a vagabond. We had a beautiful ceremony during which Paul was named the "Vagabond of L'Arche". We put a big medal of the Blessed Virgin round his neck. I gave him a paper saying that he was my friend and that I should be grateful to those who put him up and gave him food.

Paul stayed on with us a bit. But one evening I had to go

9

away and I was worried. I knew that from time to time **he** had spectacular crises of anger, and I did not want to leave him in the house during my absence. The same day, Colette had to go to Paris to see her mother and I asked her if she could take Paul with her. So it was that Paul met Colette's family.

Some days later, he left by train for the south. All went very well. Friends met him. But two days later he telephoned: "I want to go back to Paris." He's a vagabond; that is his right! He arrived in Paris, where he knew only one place. But Colette wasn't there and her mother wasn't very happy when Paul arrived unshaven and disturbed. And when, to attract attention, he pretended to throw himself out of the window, Colette's mother was frightened. She did not understand Paul's language, his call for help. The police and a nearby psychiatrist intervened. Paul was shut up in hospital.

He was put, completely naked, into a cell where he stayed for several days before we got a telephone call from the hospital, asking us to come and get him and advising us to bring more than one person because he might be dangerous. We found him completely drugged; he could hardly walk.

Paul's story is full of suffering. Born into an environment of sadness and dirt, raised in hate and discord, with never a moment of calm to bring peace to his tired heart, Paul is "abnormal", a "madman", a "delinquent". Those words! You can throw all the names you want to, but it is still a fact that Paul is Paul with his cry of distress, his sufferings, his longings, his incapacities and his difficulties in relating to the real world and to people. And people say that Paul is abnormal? Normal people are afraid of him, because he throws them into danger, into anguish. He has nothing to lose in a theft or an act of violence. Normal people, on the other hand, risk losing their goods, so they must throw up defensive barriers. Anyway, they don't want to compromise with the Pauls. Pauls should be put in the hands of specialists or of the police. Pauls are too inconvenient: hide them; remove them from sight; lock them up.

But Paul is a person, Paul is a child of God, Paul is loved by Jesus.

Isn't each man handicapped? It is false to distinguish, as we do, between "normal" and "abnormal".

The handicaps of some are more visible; for others they are hidden; their fear, their egoism, their hardness of heart, their pride, their self-satisfaction, their inability to listen. They have eyes, but they do not see the sufferings of others. They have ears but they do not hear the cries for help. They have hearts but they do not love the heart of the other who weeps.

Recently I went to a Canadian hospital. In the first rooms, I met people who were preparing to return to "normal" society. They looked at me and I said "Good morning" and they smiled slightly. Then I went to see the "very defective", the "chronic cases", who were further away. They came and took my hand and said, "My name is Robert, what is your name?" "My name is Jean, and you, what do you do?" We talked and it felt good to be with them, but I was rather sickened, because of the intolerable conditions in which they live. What can I do? I was drawn to these men who are wounded and simple. I felt this immense sadness in the depths of their hearts, and yet no barriers. Even more, by their call and their surrender, they brought down the walls in my own heart. Their sufferings, their solitude, were an invitation which made me want to stay with them, to share their lot, to be close to them, a source of liberation and peace.

Then I left them and passed again through the rooms of the "nearly normal", who gave me a pale smile. Finally, beyond the hospital fence, I went into the "normal" world, where people don't talk to me and don't smile with me; into the world where there is no compassion, no community, only people who run and don't stop for the sufferings of their brothers, for they are in a hurry, they have their business, their money to earn, and their style of life to defend.

In the so-called normal world, we look at titles and function more than at the person. We look, then we measure efficiency of action and amount of possessions rather than quality of being. People are called "Doctor", "Director", "Chairman" and so on, and often their relationships with others remain superficial and exterior, even functional. These aren't relationships between people: they are relationships between titles or functions. And there is no heart in title or in function. But a person is the heart, and the heart is compassion, tenderness, listening, understanding and union.

Over the last four years I have had the grace to visit prisons and to share with many friends in them. I am always struck by the walls, the electric doors, by the harshness in the environment; more than that, I am hurt by the stories of wounded people. Many of them took to crime at the age of fifteen; yet there is such great beauty in each one.

Réal is condemned to death in one of the prisons in Montreal and is considered a very dangerous man. But he is not; he is a wounded man and there is great beauty in him. In many ways, he is a child, with all the beauty of a child, but a child who has been deeply hurt, deeply wounded from his birth. His life is a life of rejection, frustration, violence and incarceration. He was in prison at the time when the House of Commons was talking about capital punishment. I was able to speak with him then. I was also able to follow the debate during the three days I was privileged to spend with men in the penitentiary at Drumheller. I had the impression that all the good people who were talking about capital punishment knew very little about what was really happening in the lives of those men; there seemed to be a vast wall between what was being said and what was being lived.

12

And what, finally, is murder? Yes, there is the man who wilfully takes the life of another, but there are also men who take life because they do not give. A person who possesses the goods of this world and closes his heart to those who are in need, is he not in some way a murderer if a person in need dies? If someone is capable of listening, of giving life, and he does not listen to a wounded person, who then sinks into depression and commits suicide, is not the first person a murderer? If a country is rich and wastes money on superfluous goods and does not come to the aid of other countries, then, in the brotherhood of peoples and the family of nations, is not that country a murdering country? If someone has extra room in his house and could take people in, and another dies spiritually because of overcrowding in a hospital, how far is the first a murderer?

World of suffering
misery
distress

We prefer not to see it
not to stop
If we did,
how could we live
as we did before?

Many people don't want
to visit the prisons
that's normal

If I go into the prison
I find myself before

men and women

They look at me

I look at them

Their eyes call me

I start to listen
I listen to a man

tell me what happened
why he is there

13

I discover

> he has lived in misery
> he was born into a broken family
> he was known only discord
> contact with alcoholism
> drugs, crime, violence
> he has never had a chance

And I discover
I have received so much
a family who love me
few material problems
few worries
peace

So I discover

> he is true to the logic
> of his being

truer than I am

Perhaps it's I
who should be
in prison

> he who should be free

If I had known his sufferings
I should certainly have
done worse

> So I begin to identify with him

The problem of the "normal" world is fear. We have so much fear of one another; we are afraid of meeting.

It is very easy to understand the parable of the priest and the Levite who passed by the stranger on the road who had been beaten by robbers till he was half dead. Individually and collectively, it is our own story of every day. The same is true of the story of Lazarus and the rich man. The rich man did not see Lazarus, covered with ulcers and dying of hunger. We don't see him either. We do not want to see him. So we build ghettos and call them prisons or hospitals, where the poor man is shut away. Or else we shut ourselves

14

off in our "smart" areas, into which he cannot come.

And then everything is easier. We can't see and we don't know, and that is the way we want it. It is upsetting to meet someone in misery. But Lazarus is always there, on the edges of the district, even if he isn't any longer at the door of the house.

If someone answers our "Good morning, how are you?" by saying "Things are going badly, I've lost my job," or by telling us about their grandmother who is dying, we feel ill at ease, we feel we must do something. When we ask how people are, we don't want an answer which calls us to action or to love and compassion. The other person has ignored the ritual reply of "Fine, and how are you?" which does not involve us and never commits us. When someone answers us with the truth we feel stuck, and to get ourselves unstuck we edge away: "I'm terribly sorry but I have to go somewhere. I have a meeting, I simply must run. Forgive me, but I will send a social worker along and I'm sure things will be better soon." We dissociate ourselves by sending along someone else, who, as we know, will be unable to do anything. But we are left with a clear conscience; we haven't left him alone, we have directed him to somebody else.

One of the great myths of our civilization is that of the specialist. We are always putting things onto someone else, above all when it is a matter of suffering, of misery that demands our total presence. Our immediate reaction to all sad and impossible situations is to shut our hearts, to create a world of excuses to avoid being inconvenienced.

And yet, as St. John said,

> **But if anyone has the world's goods and sees his brother in need, yet closes his heart against him, how does God's love abide in him?**
>
> **I John 3, 17**

15

We are afraid of the person in misery because he constitutes a danger to us. His poverty and his needs challenge our riches. So we raise the barriers to keep him from our sight.

The little child of three ignores those barriers and fears. Faced with the sick man, the handicapped man or the prisoner, he throws himself into his arms and plays without fear. The other begins to heal because someone treats him without fear. But the child grows up. He goes to school and then reads psychology at University. The handicapped man becomes "the case on page 159". Blinded by theory, by the handicap and the "disturbed behaviour", the psychologist tends no longer to see the person behind the handicap.

This is not to say that specialization is bad in itself. But the "non-specialists" often have a more open heart, a more universal view of life. The essential thing is to be open to the world of compassion. The wounded man needs, above all, someone who will listen to him, because in all suffering we seek first a friend who welcomes us, who appreciates us, who finds what we have to say important. Afterwards comes the time for pedagogy, the time for support which may demand a certain specialization to find the best possible solution.

Walking in the slums of Bombay, I felt in myself all these barriers which prevented me from going up to a woman whose husband earned twenty dollars a month for a family of six children. Her eldest daughter earned only five dollars a month in a plastics factory, hardly enough to pay for her transport. Think about feeding eight people on twenty dollars a month, not counting the rent, which is quite important, even in a slum!

But if I get too near this woman
    if I listen to her
    if I begin to know the names of her children
                her past
                her life
        If I identify with her

I can't go on eating as I used to
I can't accept the luxury and the waste

If I truly love
if I feel concerned
my life must change

My life must change
the life I have built for myself
must be destroyed
must be completely changed

the time I get up and go to bed
the friends I like to talk with
                go out with
                eat with in smart restaurants

the books I read
the money I have to spend

If I enter the world of touch
        the world of tender compassion
        the world of the prisoner, the handicapped, the
        hungry
my whole way of life is in danger of falling apart.

I am in danger of entering a world of insecurity.

And yet we need security
those landmarks
which let us know where we are
and perhaps let us know ourselves
                a little

If I become truly open
                open to the sufferings of others
my life will change
I will change
It's too much
I'm afraid.

So better cross the street
        not stop by the half-dead man
        not look at him
        not visit the prisons, the handicapped, the sick.

Or if I do stop
invent reasons
        not to become involved
        not to give myself
        not to touch them
        not to become committed.

Exciting theories!
Society had better change!
Abolish poverty!
I'll start a revolution
I'll solve everything
There won't be any more poor people!

Or I'll go back to my books
                to my humane or revolutionary talk
    I'll escape to drugs, to television, to eroticism
            or throw myself into hyperactivity
            work to make money
            not knowing how to spend
            on increasingly
                useless
                suicidal luxuries
            which kill
            by comfort
    I'll escape the poor, the suffering, the forsaken
    I'll flee the world of compassion.

The poor man — the weak man, the man who cries out because he is in need — is a danger to the rich man, the man who is self-satisfied and shut up in his liberty and his pride. If the rich man starts to approach the poor man, he cannot remain rich. He has to change. He has to open himself and he has to share.

The poor man is a danger to the rich man. The black man is a danger to the white man enfolded in his pride and sense of superiority. The handicapped and the weak are a danger to the able-bodied. The person in need is a danger to the one who has the goods of this world. So too the rich man is the enemy of the poor man. Yet Jesus said, "Love your enemy". We must cross over to the other world and look at Him and touch Him.

But Jesus
I can't love my enemy
I must defend myself from him

He is a danger to me
his way of life throws mine
into question

His ideas are a danger
to mine
his life is a constant challenge

So I attack
it's my defence

Or I ignore him
I refuse to listen or go near
Aggression rises
in me

Or I flee
I refuse to meet
the enemy

And yet

"Love your enemy, make peace."

2

The Kingdom Between

The Bible is the history of these two worlds and of these two enemies, Lazarus and the rich man. Jesus put Himself between these two worlds. He saw and identified with the world of the rejected, the humble and the little. He said, "Come, Live!" He came to give light to the blind, pardon to sinners and to announce a time of grace and forgiveness. He announced his message by calling all men to follow Him and to take their place between these two worlds.

Blessed are you in your poverty;
you are not shut in the false world of
convention, riches, and human security.

Blessed are you because you are gentle;
you refuse violence and aggressiveness;
you allow yourself to be led by the Spirit
into the world of tenderness and patience.

Blessed are you because you hunger and
thirst for justice; your heart beats in the
rhythm of the heart of Jesus.

Blessed are you because your heart is pure;
you do not accept compromises.

Blessed are you because you are merciful;
you attach your heart to misery;
you will receive mercy and no one will see
your sin.

Blessed are you because at all times and at
every moment you want to be an
instrument of peace; seeking unity, understanding, and reconciliation above all
things.

Blessed are you because you have allowed
your own conscience to develop;
you have not been swayed by what people
might say about you and you have acted as
a free individual;
you have accepted persecution;
you have not been afraid to proclaim
the truth.

Then Jesus turned to the world of the self-satisfied and
declared,

**Woe to you that are rich. . .that are full
now. . .that laugh now, for you shall mourn
and weep.**

Luke 6, 24

**It is easier for a camel to go through the
eye of a needle than for a rich man to enter
the kingdom of God.**

Luke 18, 25

The rich man is rich precisely because he does not know
how to give, because he does not know how to share. If he
had known how to share he wouldn't be rich any longer. He
who has shut himself into a world of defensiveness and
pride cannot enter into the kingdom of sharing. The key to
the kingdom, the only key, is openness: to open one's arms,
one's eyes, one's heart, because the kingdom of God is just
like that — the place of meeting, of communion, of peace,
and of giving.

We are ill at ease before Jesus and his Kingdom because

we feel incapable of leaving human security to follow Him. We are afraid when we consider what He might ask of us. We do not trust that His love will satisfy our deepest aspirations. We are afraid to give in to Him even a little. But still He says: "Follow me; do not be afraid; leave everything; sell everything and become, with me, a prophet of peace."

But we are rich and we feel so far away.

We feel within ourselves the sky-scrapers, the slums, the world of darkness — this mud up to the knees, up to the neck, which stops us from getting up and going forward.

We don't seem able to follow Jesus and then we are sad, even despairing. It is hard to be faced with ourselves; with our mediocrities, our cowardices, our fears and weaknesses, and all this when we feel in our hearts aspirations toward peace, universal love and the struggle for justice. It is hard to feel the weight of all the mud and mediocrity which stops us from moving.

But at Christmas a child is born to us and the angel announces, "I come to bring you good news, a great joy." For today, He who will break your chains, who will save you from yourselves, is born. (*cf.* Luke 2, 10)

It is He, Jesus, who has come to break these chains. It is He who is born and who must be born today in each one of us. He has come to save us from the mud of sin, to give us liberty and peace, so that we can follow Him between the two worlds, so that we can lead others towards the kingdom of hope.

> **Is this not the fast that I choose:**
> **to loose the bonds of wickedness,**
> **to undo the thongs of the yoke,**
> **to let the oppressed go free,**
> **and to break every yoke?**
>
> **Is it not to share your bread with the**
> **hungry, and bring the homeless poor into**
> **your house; when you see the naked, to**

cover him, and not to hide yourself from
your own flesh?

Then shall your light break forth like the
dawn and your healing shall spring up
speedily; your righteousness shall go before
you, the glory of the Lord shall be your rear
guard.

Then you shall call, and the Lord will
answer; you shall cry, and he will say,
Here I am.

If you take away from the midst of you the
yoke, the pointing of the finger and
speaking wickedness,
If you pour yourself out for the hungry and
satisfy the desire of the afflicted,
then shall your light rise in the darkness
and your gloom be as the noonday.

And the Lord will guide you continually,
and satisfy your desire with good things,
and make your bones strong;
and you shall be like a watered garden, like
a spring of water, whose waters fail not.

And your ancient ruins shall be rebuilt; you
shall raise up the foundations of many
generations;
you shall be called the repairer of the
breach, the restorer of streets to dwell in.
Isaiah 58, 6-12

Yahweh, through the mouth of Isaiah, calls us to enter
into the world of compassion. But it is Jesus who must first
break the chains which hold us in the oppression of our lust,
who must loose the bonds of the yoke of our egoism and
self-sufficiency, who will give us the freedom to love
without fear. He will feed us with His body and shelter us in
His heart. He will give us the strength and courage to go
forward into this kingdom of sharing and love between the
two worlds.

Jesus is the One who walked between the two worlds
            announcing the Good News of divine love
the One who has come to give hope
            to the sad and distressed
            but also to the self-satisfied

                    for often the rich are ignorant
                    shut in their world of possessions
                    searching for power
                    because they are afraid
                    afraid of the encounter
                    afraid of losing
                    their way of life

                    they don't know
                    they can love
                    and live in community
                    with their brothers and sisters

Jesus is the One who walked between the two worlds
            calling the poor to life
            making the rich understand
            that they are on the road
            to death
                    for where else can he be heading
                    this man who shuts himself in things
                    and riches and ambition and power?

Jesus is the One who placed Himself between
            Lazarus and the rich man
            the Levite and the poor man
            beaten by brigands lying half dead
            not far from Jericho

Jesus placed Himself between
            the poor man on his knees at the back of the temple
            who wept and dared not even look before him
            and the Pharisee up front who said to God
            "Look at me
            You must be glad to think
            You created someone
            as beautiful as me."

Jesus is the One who wants to unite
　　　these two worlds.

**That they may all be one; even as thou,
Father, art in me, and I in thee.**
　　　　　　　　　　　　　　John 17, 21

We must look at Him, and follow Him
　　　　　　　　between these two worlds
Yearning to love
hidden in the bosom of the Father
thirsting
thirsting to give life

　　　　　He calls me to walk
　　　　　between these two worlds
　　　　　with Him, in Him
　　　　　to give life

　　　　　to give my life.

He calls me to give hope, first to the small and the weak,
to those who are broken by life and by oppression. He calls
me to share my bread with them, to shelter them, to loose
the yoke of their sufferings and open them towards liberty
and confidence. He calls me to live with them, to make
known to them the love of the Father.

**Truly, I say to you, as you did it to one of
the least of these my brethren, you did it to
me.**
　　　　　　　　　　　　　　Matthew 25, 40

He calls me also to hold out my hand to the self-satisfied,
to the comfortable. He wants them in the Kingdom. It is not
a question of attacking them, but of calling them. I must not
make them too frightened, but must give them support and
help them to commit themselves in following Jesus. Once in
contact with the poor, they will become taken up by
distress; not the discomfort of a bad conscience which

refuses compassionate contact, but the distress of wounded people whom they will have seen and touched. Having seen and touched people in distress, they will begin to love, begin to dispossess themselves of their riches, begin to share.

They will no longer be able to go back, because they will feel the call to change themselves, to be reborn. They will progressively let go of their money, their way of life. They will open up, they will discover the freedom of love and sharing.

Sometimes, one has to be abrupt with the self-satisfied who refuse to move; one has to speak with a certain violence. But it is the violence of one who loves and does not crush, who wants to help the other with his difficulties, his fears and his inabilities, to break down the walls.

> **Woe to you, scribes and Pharisees, hypocrites! For you cleanse the outside of the cup and of the plate, but inside they are full of extortion and rapacity. You blind Pharisee! first cleanse the inside of the cup and of the plate, that the outside also may be clean.**
>
> **Matthew 23, 25-26**

It's no wonder that Jesus only lasted three years. If you begin to use the word "hypocrite" a certain amount, as He did, you won't last much longer, for it is a word deeply charged with emotion. To call someone a hypocrite is to say that he is using apparent virtue not for ends of love, but to dominate others, to seek pleasure and profit. A hypocrite is someone who uses the word of God for his own benefit, his own enrichment and power, and in whom there is a gap between what he says and what he lives.

Jesus is a threatening person, because He is always true. He is always in the light and there is no darkness in Him, for He is light; He is the light of the world. By His very presence, He shows up the darkness which is in me. His purity makes me become conscious of my own impurity. His truthfulness makes me become conscious of my lies and hypocrisy. His peace makes me conscious of my divisions and anguish. His welcoming of others makes me conscious of how closed I am.

Unification of our being — uniting the words we speak, the things we believe in and the life we live — is a long process, and when we stop seeking it, hypocrisy creeps in. Anybody who proclaims the word of God knows that there is always a discrepancy between what he says and what he lives. He has only the courage to announce the word if he knows it is not his own, but that of Jesus. His hope is that gradually, by the gift of the Spirit, the word he proclaims will come into and transform his own heart.

> **And making a whip of cords, he drove them all, with the sheep and oxen, out of the temple; and he poured out the coins of the money-changers and overturned their tables. And he told those who sold the pigeons, "Take these things away; you shall not make my Father's house a house of trade." His disciples remembered that it was written, "Zeal for thy house shall consume me."**
>
> **John 2, 15-17**

The anger of Jesus is even more terrifying than the anger of other men, for it is the anger of God, the anger of the Just One, who cannot stand mediocrity and injustice. He is impatient at the loss of the true meaning of the sacred, the true life of God. He is impatient with those who mock the name of God, and the things of God, to divert them to the greater comfort of man. For the message of God is not a comforting message: it is a dangerous message which threatens and accuses us, but which at the same time draws us, calls us, says to us "Come!"

The rich man sometimes needs to be traumatised by hard truth and forceful action, to break down his comfort and security and above all his indifference to and scorn and exploitation of the poor. The anger of God, like the anger of men, makes people afraid.

Faced with this anger, we begin to move. But concessions made out of fear don't have much value; they are quickly retracted. For the wall between the two worlds to fall and a new world of brotherhood to be born, it is essential that our hearts be touched. It is not a matter of beating down the rich man so that he reacts with even greater violence and feels he must build even more solid defensive walls. It is a matter of helping him penetrate, by the grace of the Spirit, into this kingdom of sharing.

Who will help me to the other side?

These two worlds are in fact at the heart of each one of us. We are full of divisions. Lazarus lives in us, as well as the rich man.

In each one of us there is the despairing, the miserable, the poor, who escapes into a world of illusions
                              of sadness
                              of death
battered by grief
mourning for life
          for hope
          for a friend who has left
                    who no longer notices
mourning a defeat

I fall into sorrow and despair
Not worth acting
          creating
          loving — that's illusion
          lacking motivation

Better stick with what I've got
a little money
a small security
mediocrity

If I die
too bad
I give up
any struggle

Many of our hearts carry
deep wounds
        wounds of indifference
                        rejection
                        hatred
                        fear
open wounds
anguish to think that someone could touch them

I'm afraid
I build a wall around me
        a wall of timidity, aggression or depression
I refuse to look at others
for fear
        they might look back

But sometimes
through a sense that comes and goes
I have the feeling
I can become
        otherwise
        I take off
        into work
        search for money
        wanting to seem
        big and strong
        through knowledge power money success

        I dream
        of my greatness
        of my richness
        of my reputation
        of everything I can be

I exist!
I am someone!

So I become
the rich man who cannot see the poor

Then one day
the balloon bursts
everything collapses
and I fall back
to the other side
of the wall
sorrow
despair
death

Yet there is also this third world in me
                    world of hope
                    world of communion
                    world of compassion
                    the call to the Kingdom

                    You hear them talking
                    of this world
                    of fraternity and peace
                    all over the place
                    They sing about it
                    some of them live it

I feel in the depths of my being
this little grain
which wants to grow
when I meet this person
when I hear that song
when I read that book
                    I want it to grow
                    I believe in it

I believe in it
but then
I don't dare
because I don't really know
what it is

There's a danger
I might not find it
and that could hurt

and after all

things weren't too bad
till now

                    So what is this whisper
                    inside me?
                    what does it mean?
                    what is it?

But after all

I don't need it
I don't believe
it's really there

and after all

better keep a foot
in the world of security
Mustn't give up completely
Mustn't lose myself
It's crazy to abandon yourself
in the arms of the Father

But very quickly you discover it isn't possible to have
a foot on each side

Oh sure
if I stay with words
I can be on both sides
because there can be a gap
between words, thought, life
I can say what I don't believe
                    I can believe what I don't want

But when it comes to life I must choose
I cannot live in two worlds
because life is like a growing tree
and my face takes form from its roots

32

The water I drink gives life
to my leaves, my flowers, my fruit
it feeds them
And the kind of birds that come to nest
will depend on the spring I drink from
If I drink living water they will be
      the doves of the Spirit

I hear in myself
    the hope
    the aspiration
    the call
but they are so rarely fulfilled
                in my hands, my look, my face
                my words
                my being
because I don't drink from a pure spring

I go on drinking water of riches
                of pleasure, prestige, and search for
                power

I go on drinking stagnant waters
                of sadness and death
                of grief and depression

So the only birds I see
are the birds of despair
crows of individualism, indifference, refusal, and pride

I feel so terribly
my inability
to meet the call to compassion and universal love
                to availability to the spirit

        And yet the hope is there
        I know it
        I feel it
        whispering deep in me

        so I try again

and again I'm afraid

I don't understand
again I fall
I don't listen
I lose all hope

> Who will help me to respond?
> Who will help me to the other side?

still so much fear
of uprooting
it stops me
giving myself

giving myself
unconditionally
to your call

fear of throwing myself
once for all
into the calm and marvellous lake
of your love

> this lake which is
> the fountain of life
> this lake which flows
> endlessly
> to bring us life

It is Jesus who walked between these two worlds and who calls us to follow Him. Jesus shows us where to find strength and hope and how to walk this road — for it is a matter of walking.

We must contemplate Jesus as He lived and, above all, follow Him, because we cannot be called disciples of Jesus Christ if we do not. And to follow Him is to put our hands in His hands, our steps in His steps. It is to take the same road and to stay on it. It is to let the fears fall away, putting our confidence in Him. So we enter gently and gradually into the world of the Beatitudes. The universe can only live, can only avoid falling into an immense conflagration of hate and death, if people start to attack the innumerable walls of fear which separate men, the universe can only live in peace if we all awaken to the importance of sharing and of welcoming others, above all the weakest, so that together we can make these two separate worlds one kingdom of brotherhood and love.

Saint Paul spoke of these two worlds when he spoke of the Jew and the Gentile. Paul is one of those who followed Jesus between the two worlds. First he was a persecutor of the disciples of Jesus. Then he was transformed by His presence and His touch. This is why he could say:

> **For he is our peace, who has made us both one, and has broken down the dividing wall of hostility, by abolishing in his flesh the law of commandments and ordinances, that he might create in himself one new man in place of two, so making peace, and might reconcile us both to God in one body through the cross, thereby bringing the hostility to an end. And he came and preached peace to you who were far off and peace to those who were near; for through Him we both have access in one Spirit to the Father. So then you are no longer strangers and sojourners, but you are fellow citizens with the saints and members of the household of God, built upon the foundation of the apostles and prophets, Christ Jesus himself being the cornerstone.**
>
> **Ephesians 2, 14-20**

Jesus calls us too
to offer our flesh
by Him and through Him
to destroy hate
proclaim the good news
create peace
reconcile the two worlds
in the kingdom of sharing

He calls us
to live this kingdom
through the Beatitudes
and no one can enter
unless he dispossesses himself

"Sell all that you have and give it to
the poor and follow me."

follow me in love

3

Jesus the Healer

"Rend the veil that prevents our sweet encounter."

I think all of us could make the cry of St. John of the Cross our own; all of us are aware at times of the veil that prevents us from knowing Jesus, prevents a limpid, perfectly clear communication with God, prevents us from knowing ourselves, from meeting people. Many of us live in delusion about ourselves, unable to see ourselves as we really are. The veil has to be broken somewhere in our deep inner being, so that we can discover who we are, accept ourselves as we are, and meet Jesus as He is. Water flowed when the rod of Moses touched the rock; in the same way, the rock of our heart has to be touched for the waters to flow, so that we can extend ourselves through living water that flows from us into others, in understanding, love and commitment.

Jesus is the healer, the One who comes to bring me life and liberate me from myself. He comes to heal me from my egoism, from my aggressiveness. He comes to heal me from my anguish.

It is a beautiful thing to meet people in deep anguish, who are able to say — like one or two men I know who are serving long prison sentences — that they are beginning to find peace. They have had an experience of death, but they feel that Jesus is gradually healing them in their frustrations, their hatreds and their fears. They have experienced all the world of hatred and darkness which can be hidden in the hearts of men, but they are moving from this world of darkness to a world of peace and light. They know what it is to pass from death to life. They know the quiet experience of the healing power of the Spirit.

When St. Paul, going from Jerusalem to Damascus, was struck and knocked off his horse, he heard a voice saying, "Saul, Saul, why do you persecute me?" His eyes were closed; he became blind. He went through a deep experience of death which was very quickly followed by an experience of life, of light. From being the persecutor, he very quickly became the persecuted. There was a quick rebirth.

Being reborn in Jesus is not so rapid for many of us. It is a quiet, gentle growth, like the growth of the child in the womb of his mother and like his gradual growth in knowledge, affection, physical strength and understanding after birth. The healing power of the Spirit is a quiet, gentle power. He makes die in us all the fears, the desire to possess, or to destroy, the hurts and the frustrations, all the power which wants to dominate. There is a growth in the power of listening, the power of compassion, of patience, of learning to wait for the hour of God. We learn to surrender to the power of the Spirit and the power of God, to stop agitating, to let God take over our lives, to abandon ourselves to the Supreme Healer.

Jesus manifests himself as He walks through Judea, when He comes to give sight to the blind, to enable the lame man to walk and the deaf to hear. All these are essentially symbols of something much deeper. He opens the eyes of the heart, so that we begin to see reality as it is, so that we see our wounded brothers, see their anguish. He opens our ears, for just as we see but are blind to reality, so we hear but do not listen. There is a fundamental healing that must take place before we really can listen to the music of reality, before we can listen to people without fear, before we can listen to the Spirit.

Jesus the Healer comes when we are conscious that we need a healer; when we become conscious of our own egoism, all the anarchy of desire, all the fears, all the cowardice and weakness, all the need for human security that incites us to possess. It is only when we become conscious of our weakness and our fears that we can begin to grow in union with the Spirit.

We know that intellectual pursuit can be flight from people. Though it can be a flight to people, it is often the opposite. The acquisition of university degrees can be flight from people — a desire to become conscious of our own power and knowledge.

The message of Jesus is folly, in human terms. Anybody who spoke like Jesus today would be considered mad, only good for a psychiatrist. His message is not for the wise; those who think that they have the power, strength and knowledge to transform the world will not understand that the folly of His message is the gift of the Spirit and the transformation of their hearts. The message is for the wounded and the little ones, the poor ones, those who are awaiting the liberator and the good news. The deeply wounded person will always recognise the liberator, because the presence of Jesus will free him, bring him peace and strength and courage, and although he cannot understand the meaning of the little piece of bread and the wine, he knows that he needs them to be transformed.

Members of our community were able to go to Lourdes with our diocesan pilgrimage, and one day we met with the Bishop and some others from the diocese in a small chapel. Just at the moment when the Bishop was called to share with us, Jean Claude stood up. In technical terms, he is mongoloid. For fifteen minutes, he talked to us of Jesus, of the poverty of Bernadette, and of prayer. There was a real manifestation of the Spirit in him, in a very moving way. Many of the people of the diocese, who don't know our group, and had always thought that people like Jean Claude were to be pitied or smothered with candies, listened to him in deep silence; they suddenly discovered that Jean Claude possessed something they did not, as he talked to us about Jesus and the cross.

I think of an old black lady of eighty, who lived alone in a broken-down area of Cleveland. She was sick: she had been vomiting all day. I went to see her and she said: "Man, I've been walking with Him for forty years, for forty years I've been walking with Him." And it was true. Her eyes were bright, something flowed from her face. While I was staring at her, amazed at the beauty in her, she burst out laughing. "You know," she said, "he must see God in me." And it was true, for God was in this little, shrivelled old lady who had been sick all day.

God reveals himself to the little and the wounded and to each of us to the extent that we accept that we are little and wounded. He liberates us from the prison of our egoisms and the prison of our comforts, from the prison of convention which prevents us from living as free human beings and even less as children of God.

> For consider your call, brethren; not many of you were wise according to worldly standards, not many were powerful, not many were of noble birth; but God chose what is foolish in the world to shame the wise, God chose what is weak in the world to shame the strong, God chose what is low and despised in the world, even things that are not, to bring to nothing things that are, so that no human being might boast in the presence of God. He is the source of your life in Christ Jesus, whom God made our wisdom, our righteousness and sanctification and redemption; therefore, as it is written, "Let him who boasts, boast of the Lord."

> I Corinthians, 26-31

There is an amazing humility in many wounded people, whether handicapped mentally or physically, and in some men and women in prison, who can come up and ask one to pray that all the hate in their hearts be dissolved. I remember April, a very beautiful black woman in a Cleveland prison who came up and asked me if I could pray that she not be sent to a certain penitentiary, well-known for its brutality and harshness, both between prisoners and between them and the administration. I told her that it would be hard for me to pray that she would not go there; that all I could pray was that she would receive the strength, the light and the love so that she might radiate love wherever she was. Then if she went to that prison, she could give solace and strength to the women who were there and needed her. I said to her, "If people like you do not go there, who will give strength and peace to the other women?" I asked if I might pray that she go where Jesus wants and that wherever she may be, she might be a source of hope for others, and she said "Yes". She said it with great freedom, and I sensed that she would be a very beautiful source of peace in that prison, if she went there. There was something so beautiful in her, particularly her quiet humility.

I visited another woman in the heart of Cleveland, who had eight or nine children. She had sores on her legs, and should have been in hospital long before. I went with Willie Mae to her broken-down house, and Willie Mae began to pray and sing, begging that strength and force would come into this woman. After about twenty minutes, as we were leaving, she said with such peaceful, childlike humility, that she felt she now had the strength to go on for a few more days, and she thanked us for praying with her.

These were people who knew their poverty, and in some ways were not frightened of it. They were turning to God and to their brothers and sisters, praying for strength, praying for the Liberator, because this is where real interior freedom begins.

"Two men went up into the temple to pray, one a Pharisee and the other a tax collector. The Pharisee stood and prayed thus with himself, 'God, I thank thee that I am not like other men, extortioners, unjust, adulterers, or even like this tax collector. I fast twice a week, I give tithes of all that I get.' But the tax collector, standing far off, would not even lift up his eyes to heaven, but beat his breast, saying, 'God, be merciful to me a sinner!' I tell you, this man went down to his house justified rather than the other; for everyone who exalts himself will be humbled; but he who humbles himself will be exalted."

Luke 18, 10-14

We must become conscious of our own infidelity, conscious of how far we are from really following the Prince of the Beatitudes. We must see how far we are from this message of Jesus: "Blessed are the poor in spirit; blessed are the meek and gentle, blessed are those who weep; blessed are the merciful; blessed are the pure in heart; blessed are those who hunger and thirst for justice; blessed are the peacemakers; blessed are those who are persecuted for the name of Jesus." We are far from this. We are far from the dynamism and energies of peacemaking, of creating new ways to become bridges in a divided world.

When the Pharisees and Scribes brought the woman taken in adultery before Jesus, they wanted to trap Him. He had been telling people to be merciful, to be understanding, to forgive, seven times seventy times, to love our enemies. "Now," said the Scribes and Pharisees, "in the law, Moses commanded us to stone such. What do you say about her?" (John 8, 5)

This is a problem we are all confronted with, one way or another — the conflict between law and spontaneity, between law and the movement of the Spirit in our hearts.

42

The law may be the one we have chosen when we entered a religious group, or accepted when we married and made a commitment to our family, or it may be the law of the land. It is very striking when one is close to prisons and begins to understand the whole evolution which brings a person to violence. It seems in a way normal for him to have entered the world of violence, because of his frustrations, his hatreds, his deprivation and his wounds. And yet, this violence is against the law of the land; someone has been hurt. There is a conflict as people look on the same act with different eyes, between the person trying to understand the violent man, and the defender of property and respect for law and order. There is a conflict between the law and what we spontaneously feel, and this has been a problem for people of all times.

The Jews come to Jesus, trying to trap Him because He is a free man and this threatens them. They want to diminish His authority by trapping Him into contradicting either the law of Moses or His own teaching. The woman is there, terrified, wounded, ashamed, and the Scribes and Pharisees are spiteful and hard. Jesus says nothing. He just starts writing on the ground. People over the ages have wondered what He was writing, but it doesn't really matter, or we would have known about it. The important thing is that He was writing, and He was writing for a very simple reason. When you are with someone who is violent, you have to find a taming process. You can start to speak very quietly, so that he is obliged to lean forward. You can offer a cigarette, and he comes forward to take it. You must somehow create openings. There is no point in talking with someone who is blocked and violent against you, because whatever you have to say will rebound.

So Jesus writes on the ground, and the Pharisees and Scribes do exactly what any of us would do: they lean forward to see what Jesus is writing about. This is the quieting process, the opening process. But they do not let themselves be opened and they continue angrily to press Jesus to say what He would do with the woman. And then,

His superb answer: "Let him who is without sin among you be the first to throw a stone at her." (John 8, 7) After they leave, the woman stands alone in front of Jesus. He says, "Woman, where are they? Has no one condemned you?" (He knows that nobody has, but Jesus likes to ask questions to which He already knows the answers.) He looks at her and smiles: "Has anyone condemned you?" She says: "No, Lord." Jesus says: "Neither do I condemn you; go and do not sin again."

It must have been a very deep meeting. If Jesus saw and loved the rich young man that He called forth, so at that moment did He love the woman. When St. Augustine talks of this meeting, he talks of the kiss of mercy and misery. The woman becomes conscious that she is in front of the Liberator, because when Jesus looks at her and says, "Do not sin again", He creates a relationship with her. She loves Him for He has saved her, and she goes away with a new force in her being. She will not sin again, because there has been a communication between the eyes of Jesus and her being, the being of Jesus and her being, and a strength comes into her.

This woman taken in adultery, we know, represents each one of us, for the whole union of love with the Spirit is a union to which I can be faithful or not. The whole history of the people of Israel is symbolized in the story of the woman who became a harlot, in the sixteenth chapter of Ezekiel. She was poor and God took her up, covered her, clothed her, cleaned her, gave her life and brought her beauty. But she turned away from Him and used this beauty and these gifts to attract men to her.

So it is with our civilization. There is no doubt that its deeper values have their source in the message of Jesus, which was propagated through time, from mouth to mouth, from Christian community to Christian community, from the rebirth at the moment of Pentecost. Our civilization bears many fruits of the message of Jesus, but we use many of these for ourselves, for our own possessions and our own power. And so the world is divided, and the rich people — or the vast majority of them — are the ones who have been baptised, and who call themselves Christians.

Yet, in lands of great poverty, as in India, you often find a greater spiritual health, a greater peacefulness, than in the rich countries. For it is in rich countries that elements of the message of Jesus have been pushed aside so that we might possess more. This is our infidelity: He gave us so much, but we have not used it to spread love, peace, unity, fellowship, mercy and understanding. The Christian churches started fighting each other, and the followers of Jesus — the Prince of Peace — threw themselves at each other's throats, each defending his own little slice of the cake of the gospels. So it was with colonialism, with the different groups wanting to take over more and more places so that they could increase their power and wealth. This is the history of mankind, abusing the gifts of God and entering into a world of harlotry, domination and division.

This is at the heart of each one of us, this meeting of Jesus with the woman taken in adultery. It is for us a very personal reality, for we have not been faithful to the quiet callings of the Spirit. We have turned away from the Lover and have used His gifts for our own power and glory.

We dare not hear this quiet whispering of the Spirit calling us forth, so that our hearts of stone may be touched and gradually transformed into hearts of flesh, opening ourselves to the wounded ones of the world, near or far, learning to love as God loves. This is the experience of the healing power of Jesus: we will be healed when we are conscious that we are adulterers, that we are filled with selfishness and have not followed this call.

When Lazarus was in the bosom of Abraham, and the rich man saw him from the place of torment, he called out:

> "Father Abraham, have mercy upon me,
> send Lazarus to dip the end of his finger in

water and cool my tongue; for I am in anguish in this flame." But Abraham said, "Son, remember that you in your lifetime received your good things, and Lazarus in like manner evil things; but now he is comforted here, and you are in anguish. And besides all this, between us and you a great chasm has been fixed, in order that those who would pass from here to you may not be able, and none may cross from there to us."

And he said, "Then I beg you, father, to send him to my father's house, for I have five brothers, so that he may warn them, lest they also come into this place of torment." But Abraham said, "They have Moses and the Prophets; let them hear them."

And he said, "No, father Abraham; but if someone goes to them from the dead, they will repent."

He said to him, "If they do not hear Moses and the Prophets, neither will they be convinced if someone should rise from the dead."

Luke 16, 24-31

So it is with us. We have not just Moses and the Prophets, we also have Jesus and we have the tradition of Jesus over the years, up to today. We can play around with the theological formulas. We can read all the books we want. But the words of Jesus are very simple. He is so simple. He announces to us that he will send us the Paraclete, the Spirit, the Paraclete who answers the cry of our being. He promises us the Paraclete because we cannot answer ourselves, and it is the Paraclete who will give us the experience of the healing power of Jesus.

These things I have spoken to you, that my joy may be in you, and that your joy may be full.

John 15, 11

When we become conscious of our own poverty, our lack of fidelity, our fears; when we become conscious that we need our Liberator, then Jesus will reveal Himself to us as the quiet and gentle Healer, drawing us from a world of darkness to a world of light, from a world of death to a world of life.

He is the Healer who loves, the Healer who in all the tenderness of His being seeks to come into us. He does not want us to be frightened of Him. Nobody could be frightened of that child, born of that young girl in Bethlehem. Nobody could be frightened of that child born of Mary in all the beauty of love. Nobody can be fearful of this man, who is in agony when He says: "My Father, if it be possible, let this cup pass from me; nevertheless, not as I will, but as thou wilt." (Matthew 26, 39) Nobody can be afraid of this man who took upon Himself the aggressiveness and the hate of the world, of the man John the Baptist calls the Lamb of God — not the Lion of Judea, not a great general, not even a great teacher or metaphysician, but the Lamb of God.

"Behold the Lamb of God, He who takes away the sins of the world." It is He who has come to heal us. He does not want us to be afraid of Him. He comes as the poor and little one, this Lamb of God who finally lets Himself be nailed to the wood, this naked man with nothing, in the unimaginable poverty of one who is condemned to death.

He is poor, surrounded by people shouting, "You saved others — now save yourself!" He does not reply.

He is poor. Who could be afraid of Him? He does not want us to be afraid. He did not even want to appear as a great person when he was dying; He did not want to appear as

47

one who did not suffer, like St. Lawrence who said, "You can turn me now, I'm cooked on this side." Some martyrs die almost laughing. Jesus did not die laughing. He died weeping.

There is poverty in the death of Jesus. We need not be afraid of Him, for He took all upon Himself. He only wanted each one of us to be transformed, touched, so that we would carry on His work, so that we would diffuse even more this message of love, this message of peace which after all is so simple.

> **And Jesus looking upon the rich young man loved him, and said to him, "You lack one thing; go, sell what you have, and give to the poor, and you will have treasure in heaven; and come, follow me." At that saying the man's countenance fell, and he went away sorrowful; for he had great possessions.**
>
> **Mark 10, 21-22**

The gospel writer talks about the sadness of the young man, but says nothing about the sadness of Jesus. But Jesus loved him. Jesus looked at him and loved him.

The heart of Jesus is the heart of a lover. When He calls people forth, it is not because He has something for them to do as workers, but because He loves them. When He calls people to become followers, it's not just the mission that He has for them, but something much deeper. It is the call of a person who loves and says, "Walk with me for I love you. You are precious in my eyes. Fear not." These words come continually through the whole of Scripture.

> **But now thus says the Lord,**
> **"Fear not, for I have redeemed you;**
> **I have called you by name, you are mine.**
> **When you pass through the waters I will be**
>   **with you;**

and through the rivers, they shall not
    overwhelm you;
when you walk through the fire you shall
    not be burned,
and the flame shall not consume you.
For I am the Lord your God,
the Holy One of Israel, your Saviour.

I give Egypt as your ransom,
Ethopia and Seba in exchange for you,
Because you are precious in my eyes
and honoured, and I love you,
I give men in return for you,
peoples in exchange for your life.
Fear not, for I am with you."

Isaiah 43, 1-5

This is the call of Jesus throughout our lives — "Come,
follow me." But it is the call of a lover. "Come, if you follow
me you will find liberty. Come."

As the rich man turns away, this love of Jesus is
wounded. Jesus is hurt, for He has in Him the power to
transform and to liberate, but He does not want to violate
people, He does not impose. He announces, He calls forth:
"If you wish, believe in me."

On Mount Sinai, when God revealed Himself to man, He
revealed Himself in power. "And the angel of the Lord
appeared to him in a flame of fire out of the midst of a bush;
and he looked, and lo, the bush was burning, yet it was not
consumed." (Exodus 3, 2) Those of us who have met with
the power of the elements — earthquakes or tempests,
typhoons or floods — have been conscious of the power of
God, the energy at the heart and source of the universe,
conscious of how small we are, how close to death each one
of us is. As God spoke to Moses, He created fear in the
hearts of men and they became conscious of their
nothingness before this power. This can draw our hearts to
admiration, to fear and obedience, to become servants of
the Almighty.

49

But Jesus does something different. He does, it's true, perform miracles which strike fear in the hearts of people. When Lazarus had been dead for four days and Jesus cried, "Lazarus, come forth!" and Lazarus teetered out of the tomb, people said: "What power this man has!" When the apostles woke Jesus up in the little boat because they were afraid of the storm and Jesus calmed the water, they were frightened by His power.

But at the same time, Jesus, with all the power he had, wept when Lazarus died, when Mary came running to him saying, "Lord, if you had been here, my brother would not have died."

> When Jesus saw her weeping, and the Jews who came with her also weeping, he was deeply moved in spirit and troubled; and he said, "Where have you laid him?" They said to him, "Lord, come and see." Jesus wept.
> John 11, 33-34

Jesus is a compassionate person, and faced with tears of death, He is moved, because the reality of death is a terrible reality. Death is at the heart of our universe, within each of us, and is our terrible anguish and poverty, as well as the fruit of sin, of that "No!" of Adam.

Jesus weeps when faced with the reality of death just as he wept over Jerusalem

> And when he drew near and saw the city he wept over it, saying, "Would that even today you knew the things that make for peace! But they are hid from your eyes. For the days shall come upon you, when your enemies will cast up a bank about you and surround you, and hem you in on every side, and dash you to the ground, you and your children within you, and they will not leave

one stone upon another in you; because you
did not know the time of your visitation."
Luke 19, 41-44

There is in Jesus, a violence, a power, and yet a strange
quietness and humility. When Jesus kneels before John,
Peter, and James, and starts to wash their feet, one can
understand Peter's reaction; any of us would have
protested. Jesus says to him: "If you do not let me wash
your feet, if you do not let me take the place of a slave, of
the least one, then you can have no part of me. We can no
longer be friends, we can no longer share together."

**Truly, truly, I say to you, a servant is not
greater than his master, nor is he who is
sent greater than he who sent him. If you
know these things, blessed are you if you do
them.**
John 13, 16, 17

In some ways, when Jesus kneels before Peter, He takes
the place of the least, of the rejected one, of the slave, of the
one the Indians call the Untouchable, the one who does the
dirty work. That is why Gandhi, in many ways, was a
follower of Jesus of the Beatitudes. He did everything he
could to change the mentality which defined people as
Untouchables. He called them the Harijhan, which in Hindi
means the "Children of God." He would go and live in their
quarter of the village so that people coming to see him
would have to come into the Untouchable area. He
identified himself with the rejected one, just as Jesus does.
This is why Jesus is enigmatic to us. This is why the
Apostles are embarrassed when He kneels and washes
their feet.

There is a quiet tenderness in Jesus, because He does not
want to be feared. He does not want to arouse admiration,
though He knows this is part of His mission. When He
changes water into wine at Cana or calls forth Lazarus from

the dead, when He heals the paralysed, or brings sight to the blind; when He multiplies the bread and people want to make Him king; then He flees. But people follow. They are in an occupied country where there are many factions and groups, and Jesus appears as a man endowed with power, who would be a good leader to throw out the conquerers. But Jesus does not want to become an earthly king.

They congregate round Him again near Capernaum, and they ask again for a sign.

> Jesus answered them, "Truly, truly, I say to you, you seek me, not because you saw signs, but because you ate your fill of the loaves. Do not labour for the food which perishes, but for the food which endures to eternal life, which the Son of man will give to you; for on him has God the Father set his seal."
>
> "Truly, truly, I say to you, it was not Moses who gave you the bread from heaven; my Father gives you the true bread from Heaven. For the bread of God is that which comes down from heaven and gives life to the world."
>
> "I am the bread of life; he who comes to me shall not hunger, and he who believes in me shall never thirst."
>
> "He who eats my flesh and drinks my blood abides in me, and I in him."
> John 6, 26-27, 32-33, 35, 56

This is something very deep and intimate in the heart of Jesus. He is saying something to the people which is a very secret reality. He wants to tell them, "I love you so much, I want to live in you." This is what love is all about. To love is to live in another person, and to carry that person in one.

Love is unity between people, a unity of sentiment and thought.

Jesus says: "If you eat my body and drink my blood, you will remain in me and I in you. Abide in me and I in you. If my words abide in you and you abide in me, ask whatever you will. Abide in me as the branch abides in the vine. Abide." This is what love is all about. To love is to abide. The lover wants to abide in the loved one as he carries the loved one in his heart.

When Jesus says, "I give you my body," it is a sign that He is living in us, that He is a lover. This food, this bread of life, is nourishment, but it is nourishment as love is nourishment. Jesus' words are the words of a lover, the words of someone who thirsts to live in people and to carry people in him. It was these words which helped people realize that He came not as a miracle worker, but as the lover, as the friend who saves and calls us forth to the Father.

"No longer do I call you servants, for the servant does not know what his master is doing; but I have called you friends, for all that I have heard from my Father I have made known to you."

John 15, 15

This is why Jesus came; to transform us, to live in us, so that we become like Him, so that we are not just cowering servants, performing the law, but a free people, freed by the Spirit, transformed by Him and in Him.

There is a wonderful phrase in the Canon of the Mass: "Grant that we, who are nourished by His body and blood, may be filled with His Holy Spirit, and become one body, one spirit in Christ."* Filled with the spirit which comes to us through Jesus, and through His body and blood, He takes our hearts of stone and teaches us to love as He loves.

* Eucharistic Prayer III

As He teaches us to love as He loves, He makes of us one body, the body which is His church, the mystical body, not just the union of juxtaposed realities, but the union of people who, united in the Spirit, have become one body, the body of Christ.

People want someone to admire and to follow, but often they refuse the folly of the lover. When He offers them His body as food and His blood to drink (*cf* John 6) they refuse. They cannot accept this folly. They start to leave Him, one after the other, and Jesus looks at Peter and says: "Will you also leave me?" That extraordinary, plaintive phrase is charged with emotion and sadness, because Jesus loves and because people do not understand this healing love.

Jesus does not impose; He does not try to hold people back. He does not even try to mitigate what he has said, blunting it with compromise. He doesn't put water into the wine and dilute His message. Like all lovers, He is patient and calls forth. This is the word of Jesus: "Come, I do not impose. But come, follow me. Let me touch your inner being, heal the scars of hardness, egoism and cowardice and call you forth to life and liberation."

4

Grow

Jesus said to Peter and John and James, "Come, come, follow me." And they left their little fishing boats, their only means of subsistence; they left their old father Zebedee; they left everything and they followed Him. They put their hands in the hand of Jesus to grow in Him.

As we look at the lives of these men — very physical, very real men — we see beautiful growth in them. Jesus does not transform immediately the temperament of someone like Peter. He purifies him, He guides him, transforming him slowly and beautifully into that man who was ready to die for Him. In many ways, the story of Peter is our story; he represents many of us.

He is a strange man — highly emotional, strong and weak at the same time. Sometimes he is completely ridiculous and sometimes he is filled with nobility, meeting a situation with great beauty. In many ways he is filled with human presumptuousness — a weak man pretending to be strong.

> **Then Simon Peter, having a sword, drew it and struck the high priest's slave and cut off his right ear. The slave's name was Malchus. Jesus said to Peter, "Put your sword into its sheath; shall I not drink the cup which the Father has given me?"**
> **John 18, 10, 11**

55

Here is Jesus, surrounded by soldiers, being taken away. Peter either has to be a really bad shot, missing the head and getting the ear, or else he is cowardly and fearful. And whose ear does he get? He doesn't attack the Roman soldiers. He attacks the slave of the high priest, the most defenceless person of all. You just have to put yourself in the situation to see how ridiculous Peter is, how frightened he is.

And this is Peter — a complete fool, poor, feeble, filled with fear and unrest, yet with this naiveté of heart.

When Jesus kneels at his feet, Peter says. "No, no. You don't wash my feet." And then when Jesus says if He doesn't, Peter will not longer be His friend, Peter explodes, "Then wash my hands and my feet and my head— give me a shower." He is always going to extremes.

> **And he began to teach them that the Son of man must suffer many things, and be rejected by the elders and the chief priests and the scribes, and be killed, and after three days rise again. And he said this plainly. And Peter took him, and began to rebuke him. But turning and seeing his disciples, he rebuked Peter, and said, "Get behind me Satan! For you are not on the side of God, but of men."**
>
> **Mark 8, 31-33**

Peter is playing the big man, telling Jesus it just isn't possible that He should die. He does not realize the importance of what Jesus is saying, that Jesus is saying "I love you and I want to give you my life. For there is no greater love than that of the man who gives his life for his friends." Peter doesn't understand the secret movement of love, the secret movement of life. He doesn't really understand Jesus, and he wounds Him, and yet there is something very beautiful in his loyalty and even in his disloyalty.

56

> But when the disciples saw him walking on the sea, they were terrified, saying, "It is a ghost!" And they cried out for fear. But immediately he spoke to them, saying, "Take heart, it is I; have no fear." And Peter answered him, "Lord, if it is you, bid me come to you on the water." He said "Come." So Peter got out of the boat and walked on the water and came to Jesus; but when he saw the wind, he was afraid, and beginning to sink he cried out, "Lord save me." Jesus immediately reached out his hand and caught him, saying to him, "O man of little faith, why did you doubt?"
>
> **Matthew 14, 26-31**

You can just see a sort of smile on Jesus's face as He says, "Come!" And there is Peter, splashing about in fright. This is Peter — a child, sometimes a bit spoilt.

> And taking with him Peter and the two sons of Zebedee, he began to be sorrowful and troubled. Then he said to them, "My soul is very sorrowful, even to death; remain here and watch with me." And going a little farther, he fell on his face and prayed, "My Father, if it be possible, let this cup pass from me; nevertheless, not as I will, but as thou wilt."
> And he came to the disciples and found them sleeping; and he said to Peter, "So, could you not watch with me one hour? Watch and pray that you may not enter into temptation; the spirit indeed is willing, but the flesh is weak."
>
> **Matthew 26, 37-41**

Peter is a frightened man, frightened when Jesus is before Caiaphas and it is evident that He will very soon be put to death. His slashing out at Malchus is the action of a frightened man, a weak man, who has put his confidence in Jesus because of His strength, because of His beauty, because of His word. Yet this belief is very weak, like that of many of us. We can believe in Jesus, but our belief is weak. We are weak people.

> **Now Peter was sitting outside in the courtyard. And a maid came up to him, and said, "You also were with Jesus the Galilean." But he denied it before them all, saying, "I do not know what you mean." And when he went out to the porch, another maid saw him, and she said to the bystanders, "This man was with Jesus of Nazareth." And again he denied it with an oath, "I do not know the man."**
> **After a little while the bystanders came up and said to Peter, "Certainly you are also one of them, for your accent betrays you." Then he began to invoke a curse on himself and to swear, "I do not know the man." And immediately the cock crowed. And Peter remembered the saying of Jesus, "Before the cock crows, you will deny me three times."**
> **And he went out and wept bitterly.**
>
> Matthew 26, 69-75

Just imagine the feelings of John when he hears Peter say, "I do not know him." Peter had been with John and James at the transfiguration and had seen Jesus white as snow. And they had been together with Him just shortly before, in agony with Him, and they had eaten for the first time His body and His blood. You can sense the feelings of someone like John, who cannot understand what is going through Peter's frightened mind.

And then the cock crows, and Peter remembers what Jesus said. And Jesus turns round and looks at Peter.

Peter breaks down and weeps bitterly.

And you can imagine Peter weeping. He doesn't just have a few tears trickling down his cheeks. He howls. He is an intense man, in his poverty and his beauty.

And sometimes he has great beauty. When Jesus has just announced his folly of love, that he who eats His body and drinks His blood will abide in Him and He in them, people start to turn away, thinking He has gone mad.

> **After this many of his disciples drew back and no longer went about with him. Jesus said to the twelve, "Do you also wish to go away?" Simon Peter answered him, "Lord, to whom shall we go? You have the words of eternal life; and we have believed, and have come to know, that you are the Holy One of God."**
>
> **John 6, 66-69**

It's a beautiful reply. "You may be mad, but you're the only sane mad person I've ever met. You're the only one I've felt to have the strength and the love and the authority of the word of God. To whom shall we go, to whom shall we turn to quench this thirst for the infinite, for love and for truth, in a world where there is so much hypocrisy, so much mediocrity, so much compromise? With all the insanity of your doctrine, you have the words of eternal life." Here is the beauty of Peter, the strength of Peter.

In the same way, when Jesus asks his disciples who, for them, is the Son of Man: "Who do you say that I am?" And Peter answers, "You are the Christ, the Son of the living God." (Matthew 16, 15-16)

This weak man is sometimes filled with great force and strength in the Spirit. He proclaims more than he himself is capable of proclaiming, for it is the Father who has revealed the truth to him.

And Jesus turns to him: "Blessed are you, Simon Peter. For flesh and blood have not revealed this to you, but my Father who is in heaven."

This is the beautiful Peter, with his weakness, his poverty, his boyishness, and his strength. Later on, when the Spirit comes into him on Pentecost, there is the transformed Peter, the strong Peter.

> And when Peter saw it he addressed the people, "Men of Israel, why do you stare at us, as though by our own power or piety we had made him walk? The God of Abraham and of Isaac and of Jacob, the God of our fathers, glorified his servant Jesus, whom you delivered up and denied in the presence of Pilate, when he had decided to release him. But you denied the Holy and Righteous One, and asked for a murderer to be granted to you, and killed the Author of life, whom God raised from the dead. To this we are witnesses. And his name, by faith in his name, has made this man strong whom you see and know; and the faith which is through Jesus has given the man this perfect health in the presence of you all."
>
> Acts 3, 12-16

This is a strong Peter, a Peter who has been healed and is ready to be imprisoned for Jesus. He becomes a threat, whether inside jail or outside. He is no longer weak because he is filled with the Spirit, the Spirit which moved in him when he announced, "You are the Christ, Son of the Living God!" or when he said, "You have the words of eternal life; to whom shall we go?"

But he still remains Peter. It is very much Peter to be crucified upside down. Tradition has it that he felt he was not worthy to be crucified as Jesus was, and though it can't really matter when you are being crucified which way **up** you are, it is still very much Peter to go head down. This is his temperament, which the Spirit hasn't completely changed. It's still Peter, with his weakness and his beauty, his strength, his fear and yet his intense love for Jesus.

John is very different, though he has some of the same characteristics as Peter. In some ways, he is strong and violent, but above all he is filled with tenderness and delicacy. You just have to read his Gospel or his Epistles to sense the extraordinary finesse of his intelligence; he senses deeper than the facts, and yet his feet are always firmly on the ground.

John is precise. In his writings, he brings in small details, like the name of the slave whose ear Peter cut off, or the exact day on which something happened. He situates himself in time and space.

He brings out the reality of Jesus, an incarnated Jesus, present physically, with His need for food and rest.

> **Jacob's well was there, and so Jesus, wearied as he was with his journey, sat down beside the well. It was about the sixth hour.**
>
> **John 4, 6**

It is John, too, who brings out the fact that Jesus ate the fish and the bread, even after His Resurrection. John is a highly intelligent and perspicacious person, able in the Spirit to discern the message of God through facts; he is also very close to reality, to space and time.

Yet he has moments of violence. When they go two by two into a village and the people do not receive the word, John says to Jesus, "Lord, do you want us to bid fire to come down from heaven and consume them?" (Luke 9, 54) But Jesus turned and rebuked him, for He did not come to destroy people but to save.

John calls himself the "well beloved disciple", "the disciple that Jesus loved". One might wonder whether he waited until the other disciples were dead to write this, whether he might have been a bit afraid of their reactions. But he has such a sense of delicacy and of truth. And the other disciples knew that Jesus loved John in a very special way.

When Jesus announces during the Last Supper that He is going to be betrayed by one of them, Peter who is on his right side, turns to John and signals that he should ask who this will be. Peter is afraid to ask the question himself because he doesn't feel that Jesus will answer, so he wants John to ask.

> One of his disciples, whom Jesus loved, was lying close to the breast of Jesus; so Simon Peter beckoned to him and said, "Tell us who it is of whom he speaks." So lying thus, close to the breast of Jesus, he said to him, "Lord, who is it?" Jesus answered, "It is he to whom I shall give this morsel when I have dipped it."
>
> John 13, 23-26

This very intimate little scene, during the last moments, shows the quality of the presence of John in Jesus. This little word in Greek (ἐν τῷ κολπῳ) "lying close to the breast", to the heart, of Jesus expresses so much. This same word is used one other time by St. John:

> For the law was given through Moses; grace and truth came through Jesus Christ. No one has ever seen God; the only Son, who is in the bosom of the Father [εἰς τὸν κόλπον], he has made him known.
>
> John 1, 17, 18

It is the same Greek expression, "inside the Father, in

the intimacy of the Father". The Son can reveal the Father because He is in Him, because they love each other.

And so it is with John. He will make Jesus known because he is in Him; his resting on Jesus is the exterior sign that he is inside Him, that Jesus has revealed the secrets of the Father to him. This is the delicate John, John the Lover, John who suffers deeply, particularly at these last moments; and this is why he is resting on the heart of Jesus.

You can sense the emotion in each of the disciples when Jesus for the first time takes the bread, breaks it and gives it to each one. "Take ye this. Eat it, for it is my body. Drink the chalice, the blood of salvation. Drink my blood." There must have been such silence. These men have recognized the situation as dangerous for a year or more. The Scribes and Pharisees have been trying to get rid of Jesus; there have been times when they have even thrown stones at Him. The disciples have not been afraid because Jesus is there. But now they sense that He is to be taken away from them. This is what Jesus actually says: "It is when I go that I will send you the Paraclete. He will give you force and strength. I shall not leave you orphans." They are moved — the more because they sense what is going to happen and that they are going to have a very special role.

> **When the Spirit of truth comes, he will guide you into all the truth; for he will not speak on his own authority, but whatever he hears he will speak and he will declare to you the things that are to come. He will glorify me, for he will take what is mine and declare it to you. All that the Father has is mine; therefore I said that he will take what is mine and declare it to you.**
>
> **John 16, 13-15**

Then Jesus goes onto the Mount of Olives, followed by Peter, John and James. They are filled with emotion. Only a week before, Jesus had been proclaimed King as He rode through Jerusalem on a donkey. Now it seems the situation will be reversed. This is the emotion which fills them and tires them: they fall asleep.

And then Judas arrives, Judas who walked with Him. It is a terrible thing for the heart to discover that a brother has betrayed the leader; you just have to talk to men who were with the French Resistance during the war to sense their deep hurt when one of their number betrayed another. We can feel the deep suffering of a man like John, when Judas, with whom the disciples had lived for three years, who had shared with them, who had seen what Jesus had done, put Him into the hands of the Scribes and Pharisees — worse, into the hands of the Roman conquerors, whom the Jews despised.

After that, some hours later, it is Peter, saying he does not know Jesus. You can understand the confusion of John, this poet, this highly sensitive man, who has all the vulnerability of one who loves.

Later, as he walks alone and aimlessly, for Peter has fled and the others have disappeared, he meets Mary. He sees the face of this woman which is so like that of her Son, for it was from Mary alone that Jesus inherited his human physical characteristics. When John sees her, he finds strength. It couldn't be otherwise, for he senses Jesus in her, and she becomes a source of strength for him.

And so it is that he finds himself with her at the foot of the cross when Jesus is dying, amid all the harshness of the screaming crowd. There are very few of them present during these three hours of solitude — just Mary of Magdala, Mary the wife of Clopas, Mary the mother of Jesus, and John himself. It is when Jesus is very close to death that He turns to Mary, the silent and compassionate one, the woman whose heart has been opened up to all men by Jesus himself, through the love He has given her, which is the love of God for all men. In His quiet strength of compassion, Jesus looks at her and says: "Woman, here is your son." You can sense how John must feel when he hears this, when he hears "Here is your Mother." "How can I be her son? How can I replace you? It isn't possible, I'm not you!" You can sense that if it hadn't been during these last moments, John would have reacted as Peter did when Jesus knelt to wash his feet.

But these are the last moments of Jesus. So John becomes Jesus for Mary.

> **And from that hour the disciple took her to his own home.**
>
> > **John 19, 27**

Two or three weeks later, John tells us in the 21st Chapter of his gospel, that he and some of the disciples were with Peter, who suggested that they go fishing. All night they toiled but caught no fish. Just as dawn is breaking, Jesus appears. He is one hundred yards away, standing on the beach and he tells them to throw out their nets again. The nets immediately filled. They have a large haul. It is John, the Lover, who recognizes Jesus. "It is the Lord!" he cries out, and Peter, the impetuous one, jumps into the water, and rushes to Him.

> **When they had finished breakfast, Jesus said to Simon Peter, "Simon, son of John, do you love me more than these?" He said to him, "Yes, Lord, you know that I love you." He said to him, "Feed my lambs." A second time he said to him, "Simon, son of John, do you love me?" He said to him, "Yes, Lord; you know that I love you." He said to him, "Tend my sheep." He said to him the third time, "Do you love me?" And he said to him, "Lord, you know everything; you know that I love you." Jesus said to him, "Feed my sheep."**
>
> > **John 21, 15-17**

65

Then, after prophesying about Peter's death, Jesus says to him, "Follow Me". At that moment, Peter turns and sees John also following, and in a moment of rather understandable curiosity, he says to Jesus, "What about him?" Jesus has just confided to Peter a mission. Peter wonders what mission He is going to confide to this other disciple, for whom He has special love, and who was faithful to the Cross. Instead of just following Jesus as he'd been asked, Peter squints at John. "What's going to happen to him? What place has he?" Jesus gives a beautiful answer. "What is it to you if he remains until I come?" In reality these rather enigmatic words mean, "It's none of your business."

There is a tendency for each of us to look at others, wanting to imitate them or criticise them, instead of following Jesus. Instead of obeying our own call, we seek approbation, or we pretend to be other than we are. St. Paul tells us in Corinthians that in the Church, each has his special gifts and each must be fulfilled according to these gifts. The lay person can easily criticise the priest, and the priest, the bishop. We must not condemn the speck in the eye of another when we have a log in our own. We must learn to grow in our own call and follow Jesus. Peter has his mission. John has his. One is not greater than the other. Each has a service to render and each must grow according to the music of his own being. Thus we will become one Body, the Body of Christ.

5

Become a Shepherd

Jesus does not come like a doctor, to heal us and then to leave us. This healer is a shepherd, the good shepherd who teaches us to walk in the paths of the Beatitudes. As the healer calls us to heal, so the shepherd calls us forth to be shepherds.

Each of us is a shepherd, in some way. A parent is a shepherd to his child, a teacher to a student, a priest to a parishioner; a friend can often be a shepherd to a friend, for they guide each other. All of us are called to shepherdhood in some way for we are all responsible one to another.

It is important to see how Jesus is a shepherd, to discover how we should be shepherds. One of the reasons that there is a good deal of confusion in this world is precisely because there are too few good shepherds, deeply committed to the flock, deeply committed to people. Shepherdhood is a commitment to people, whatever may happen. They may be well, they may fall sick, but they are *my* people and they need me to grow in love, in peace and in gift of self; they are my flock and if they are wounded I too am wounded.

It is important for us to delve a little into the meaning of shepherdhood, to understand the commitment that it implies, to discover the responsibility each one of us has, whatever our age, whatever our function. Each of us is called to fidelity, to commitment, even if this is simply the commitment of friend to friend. The friend senses the friend

67

who is really committed. There are false friends who are there to laugh when we laugh, but not to weep when we weep. There are false friends who are there to profit from our intelligence or our possessions, but who disappear when we are sick or destitute or rejected.

> Truly, truly, I say to you, he who does not enter the sheepfold by the door but climbs in by another way, that man is a thief and a robber; but he who enters by the door is the shepherd of the sheep. To him the gatekeeper opens; the sheep hear his voice, and he calls his own sheep by name and leads them out. When he has brought out all his own, he goes before them, and the sheep follow him, for they know his voice. A stranger they will not follow, but they will flee from him, for they do not know the voice of strangers.
>
> John 10, 1-5

Jesus used this image of the shepherd, but they did not understand what he was saying.

> So Jesus again said to them, "Truly, truly, I say to you, I am the door of the sheep. All who come before me are thieves and robbers; but the sheep do not heed them. I am the door; if any one enters by me, he will be saved, and will go in and out and find pasture. The thief comes only to steal and kill and destroy; I came that they may have life, and have it abundantly. I am the good shepherd. The good shepherd lays down his life for the sheep. He who is a hireling and not a shepherd, whose own the sheep are not, sees the wolf coming and leaves the sheep and flees; and the wolf snatches them and scatters them. He flees because he is a

hireling and cares nothing for the sheep. I am the good shepherd; I know my own and my own know me, as the Father knows me and I know the Father; and I lay down my life for the sheep. And I have other sheep, that are not of this fold; I must bring them also, and they will heed my voice. So there shall be one flock, one shepherd. For this reason the Father loves me, because I lay down my life, that I may take it again. No one takes it from me, but I lay it down of my own accord. I have power to lay it down, and I have power to take it again; this charge I have received from my Father."

John 10, 1-18

This is the good shepherd.

The word of the Lord came to me: "Son of man, prophesy against the shepherds of Israel, prophesy and say to them, even to the shepherds, Thus says the Lord God: Ho, shepherds of Israel who have been feeding yourselves! Should not shepherds feed the sheep: You eat the fat, you clothe yourselves with the wool, you slaughter the fatlings; but you do not feed the sheep. The weak you have not strengthened, the sick you have not healed, the crippled you have not bound up, the strayed you have not brought back, the lost you have not sought, and with force and harshness you have ruled them. So they are scattered, because there was no shepherd; and they became food for all the wild beasts. My sheep were scattered, they wandered over all the mountains and on every high hill; my sheep were scattered over all the face of the earth, with none to search or seek for them."

Ezekiel 34, 1-6

These are the bad shepherds.

Jesus said to Peter: "Feed my sheep. Feed my lambs."

To feed a flock, to feed the lambs, you must know their needs. If the shepherd does not know the flock, he will give it food which it vomits and rejects. Shepherds have stuffed down dogma when the people needed something else; they have stuffed down law, when they needed commitment, tenderness and understanding. The flock must receive the right kind of food to call them forth, to call forth the Spirit in them. They need someone who is really attentive to their deep needs.

If you are to know the needs of the flock, you must get close to them, live with them, listen to them and understand them. You must listen to their needs, their aspirations and their hopes, and begin to sense the type and quality of food that will really nourish their being and their hearts.

> I am the good shepherd; I know my own and
> my own know me, as the Father knows me
> and I know the Father; and I lay down my
> life for the sheep.
> **John 10, 14-15**

Love for the flock does not mean giving them ice cream on holidays. It means that we are prepared to sacrifice our reputation, to sacrifice ourselves. It means that we are committed to them and that we won't slide away under the cover of some law or pretext which is really a defence against commitment.

The flock quickly sense somebody who is deeply concerned for them, somebody who is open, ready to listen at any moment. A shepherd who allows the sheep to knock at his door only between two and four, Monday to Friday, is not a good shepherd. The flock won't come between two and four, Monday to Friday. They will come between midnight and one in the morning on Saturday. They will always come when one doesn't want them, when one is busy, or in the middle of the night when they are suffering; and they will come then because they sense that the shepherd is deeply concerned for them and for their needs. The good shepherd will always be welcoming, always open, because he is concerned for his sheep and ready to lay down his life for them. The good shepherd has no holiday; when he rests he carries his people with him.

When Jesse Jackson spoke to two thousand inner city people in downtown Chicago, he said: "My people are humiliated. My people are wounded."

Mother Teresa of Calcutta says: "My people are hungry."

"My people." There is no rest when we have "my people".

These are good shepherds, for they are committed to *their* people.

When one of his people is wounded, or in danger of suicide, or is not growing; when one of his people is in a critical state and needs special nourishment, the shepherd does not go on holiday. The sheep sense the difference between the shepherd who is really concerned for them and the hireling who slips away as soon as there is a problem. Children sense when their parents sacrifice a rise in position so that the father may be more present in the home. People sense when the shepherd is concerned for the whole flock, not just for one or two who are more "interesting". Some teachers can be more concerned with the two or three apparently more intelligent students; they fail to give enough attention to the little ones, the crippled, the hurt and the wounded, who in fact need their care even more than the others.

> **I came that they may have life, and have it abundantly.**
>
> **John 10, 10**

71

Some shepherds are only happy when their flock is orderly, when it doesn't make too much noise and walks in a straight line. This is not good for people. The good shepherd is the one who calls his flock to liberty, each person finding his uniqueness, creativity and commitment.

This can bring a sort of chaos to the flock, because as soon as you call people to greater liberty they will all be moving in different directions. And this can sometimes be frightening.

But when you go into a classroom and things are very neat, or into a dormitory and find the room very tidy, with nothing on the floor, nothing pinned up on the walls, there's something wrong. Because people are not orderly by nature. They crave for creativity and liberty. They need to have things on the wall and perhaps their beds unmade and the place a bit scruffy. This is reality; this is home; this is people.

People are not terribly neat and orderly; they are not machines to be polished up so that the shepherd can collect praises for *his* tidiness, *his* capacity. People growing in liberty do not all have the same haircuts and look the same and wear the same smiles. Each one is different, each one is growing in his own way, in positive action, and in love. The flock will sense if the shepherd is demanding order because he is scared of people, if he is just seeking his own power and glory.

The shepherd must be prepared to compromise himself for his flock, for he loves his flock. He is committed to each member, whatever his intelligence or his beauty or his age. He knows each one by name and he senses the individual needs of each.

This is why it is important for the shepherd to be present to each member of the flock in a special way, saying something personal to each one. This is why he must know each by name, in so far as the name represents the deep person and his deep needs.

The good shepherd speaks the language of the flock. Some shepherds do not, for they do not know all the ways the flock has of communicating. This does not mean that someone working with prisoners has to use spicier language than he normally would. But the prisoner must sense that the shepherd really understands him, for it is only then that the shepherd will be able to nourish him.

The shepherd must be continually creative, for this is commitment towards people. When you love, you create and re-create. When you are in deep communion with someone who is in need, then you create ways of responding to his need.

This is the extraordinary role of the shepherd: to listen to the flock without fear, to understand their language, to give to each according to his need; to be wounded when one of the flock is wounded, to be in anguish when one of them is in anguish, to seek out the one who has gone astray and bring him back, to be firm when it is necessary to be firm.

This cannot be done without a movement of the Spirit, without the grace of the Spirit. It is one of the things we must yearn for: that the Spirit of God will come into each one of us and form our beings so that we are capable of becoming good shepherds, willing to give our lives for the flock. For today, more than at any time, the flock senses if the shepherd is authentic. If they sense that he is not, they will not follow. They will sense very quickly the discrepancy between his words and his life and actions; they will sense when the words do not flow from his being.

We must learn to grow in shepherdhood. The birth in love and in the Spirit begins when there is a meeting with a real shepherd, a disciple of Jesus, who transmits love, hope and faith, and who calls forth by his words, his attitudes and his being. The relationship between spreading the word of God and shepherdhood is so intense that if shepherds begin to act like hirelings, the flock will begin to disperse, looking for other pastures.

It is when people are not taught to pray and to enter into the mystical movement of Christianity, when they are not called forth to experience real love, that they turn to other pastures which do not really nourish. They turn away because they have not learned from their shepherd how to communicate with God, how to listen to the Spirit, how to discern the things which are of God and the things which are not. They have not received that which is essential to nourish their thirst for the Eternal and for the liberty which comes from Jesus. They do not know this truth which will set them free, the Spirit of God who liberates from fear and from law. They do not know how the Spirit will teach freedom so that they may grow in love and commitment, loving truth, refusing all the compromise that brings shadows and darkness upon the light.

If people do not sense this force of light in the shepherd, they will turn to other pastures, whether these are drugs, a world of violence and revolution or of other political theories, or the seeking of relationships only through sexuality. If there is no real pasture, people will die of depression, of starvation. They will die thirsting.

The good shepherd lays down his life for the sheep.

Maria Carolina de Jesu lived in the slums of Sao Paulo and wrote in a diary every day. "Today," she wrote, "is Sunday. The priest came to say mass. He preached to us and he said, 'God loves the poor so much.' I wonder how it is, then, that his minister spends only half an hour a week with them?" A shepherd is ready to live with his flock, ready to weep and suffer with his flock.

I remember a woman with a very retarded son of fifteen. All his life she had been washing him, feeding him, looking after him. A priest of the parish came to visit her and said. "This is the cross you must bear. I'll pray for you." But he never once came back to offer his services to the mother so that she could rest for the first time in fifteen years. It would have been better for him to say nothing, but simply to weep with the mother, so that she could feel compassion, feel she was understood. We can easily spout words which are a barrier rather than a communion, a gift of love.

Only Jesus can heal us of our egoism and give us the strength, the love, the patience and the tenderness, the understanding and the ability to listen to wounded people. Only He can teach us to become good shepherds. Only He can transform our hearts of stone into hearts of flesh, so that we are not afraid to say, "You are my people and I love you and I am committed to you."

> Love bears all things, believes all things, hopes all things, endures all things.
> I Corinthians 13, 7

6

Share Together

> **A new commandment I give you, that you
> love one another; even as I have loved you,
> that you also love one another. By this all
> men will know that you are my disciples, if
> you have love for one another.**
>
>

John 13, 34-35

Jesus heals people and then calls them forth together. He
calls forth Peter, John, Mary of Magdala, Paul. And He asks
those He has healed and called forth to join together, live
together, be together. He desires that those He has called
forth, and in whom He has put His Spirit, be united as the
Father and the Son are united. He desires that their love
for one another be something so special that people will
know by it that they are His disciples.

Jesus calls His friends to community, where they live and
share together. They are called in their unity and love for
one another to be a sign of and a witness to something very
special — the life of the Spirit, a rebirth, the good news.

> **By this all men will know that you are my
> disciples, if you have love for one another.**
>
>

John 13, 35

We know that we need brothers and sisters if we are to
grow in the Spirit. They help us by the way they live; they
encourage and strengthen us. We also know that it is easier
more often to pray when we are together than when we are

alone. Community is one of the most beautiful realities — brothers and sisters loving and being together. It is also one of the most difficult to accomplish.

Living together is difficult for human beings. Goldfish seem to manage it — you rarely see head-on collisions. Cows seem to manage all right in the same pasture — at least until the bull comes along. But put ten men together in a house and very quickly you have a hotel. Put ten women together and you soon have problems, though these are nothing to the problems you get when you put five men and five women together.

Once together, we very quickly start to squabble. We each want more than the others. We get aggressive because one of our number irritates us. Tensions arise, and then everyone starts to be very polite to hide their fear of those tensions. You can sense the coldness as people slide down corridors not daring to look at each other for fear of an explosion, or bury their head in a book when another goes past.

Yet as soon as you go into some homes you can sense a peace, an openness, a welcome, in the meeting of eyes and the smile that communicates without words.

Few people seem to know the laws of community. Community takes a long time to form. It takes a long time for barriers to drop, for mutual confidence to grow, for non-verbal communication to become more important than words. A community is only a community when most of the people in it have made the passage from "the community for me" to "me for the community". A community is only a community when most of the people in it are conscientiously trying to seek the fulfilment, peace and happiness of every other member of it.

> Truly, truly, I say to you, he who receives any one whom I send receives me; and he who receives me receives him who sent me.
> John 13, 20

There are two enemies of community for us: those people we call our enemies and those we call our "friends."

The enemy is the one who rubs me the wrong way; the one I disagree with, the one I criticise or who criticises me. Our enmity can be theological or even liturgical — there are more battles over liturgy than you would think possible. The enemy is the one who annoys me because his background or language are not the same as mine. He is the one who is always complaining that the soup is too hot or too cold. He is the one who always wants exactly the television programme that I do not. The enemy is the one I cut off, the one who ceases to exist for me, and he can be found in every home and every community.

This is to be expected, because God does not call together groups of people who are naturally adapted to one another. He calls people who are very different in their origins, customs and ways of thinking and He asks them to live together because they believe in Jesus Christ. Yet enmity brings destruction of community, for where there is enmity there are factions. Community means that most of the people are seeking to love and to find the fulfilment of every other person in that community, whatever their origins, their liturgical preferences or favourite television programmes.

The other enemy of community can be human friendship and sympathy. It brings destruction if it means the grouping together of people of the same background and aspirations, to close themselves off from other members of the community. It brings destruction if it does not open the group to all the other members of the community.

The road to community is the passage towards death to oneself and the rebirth of love, and that is a long road. It means the passage from our own interests to those of the community; the passage from my choice for me to my choice for others; the passage, Passover, Easter, from egoism to love. It is bound to be painful and hard; it is bound to bring some tenseness and aggressiveness. We all fear death, and so we are bound to struggle, until gradually the Spirit of God comes and transforms us into lovers of all who are in the community.

People who have lived alone normally find their first month in community a great joy. Everyone around them seems to be a saint; everyone seems so happy. Then in the second month, everyone is a devil. Everyone has mixed motives for whatever he does, everyone is something of a hypocrite, everyone is so greedy that he takes just the piece of meat I had my eye on. They talk when I want to be silent and when I want to talk they cut me off with their long, silent looks. It's a conspiracy.

In the third month, they are neither saints nor devils. They are people, who have come together to strive and to love. They are neither perfect nor imperfect, but like everyone else a mixture of the two. They are people who are growing, and that means the good is in the growth and the bad is what prevents growth.

This is reality. We are people who have come together to share our poverty, our hopes, our aspirations and our desires, and to grow in the Spirit. We must move quickly into accepting this reality, into accepting that all of us are wounded by sin and by egoism. Unfortunately, the second "month" — this time element is of course just a symbol and this can take ten years to arrive — is too much for many people and they run away.

We must accept that the growth from egoism to love, from community for myself to myself for community, is a long and sometimes a hard road, paved with joys and sufferings. It begins simply.

It begins by accepting our differences, and by beginning to know one another. What brings this member of the community peace? What hurts him? What brings him out of or plunges him into depression? What calms him, what irritates him? All this is important when you are living with someone. You must know what will help him to be at peace and to live in the spirit of love.

Some people need to be left alone when they are in depression. Don't go up to them and start pawing them, because they might explode. Others need attention; they need a cup of tea, to be drawn into conversation, a word of gentleness.

You can only know who needs which when you have lived with them for some time. It takes time to know their needs, their call, their thirst. It takes time to know the little things that can hurt them. Some people who come to visit us at L'Arche have the knack of saying the wrong thing, of wounding through their lack of sensitivity. They don't realize that every word can either bring peace and call forth, or can wound and throw up barriers. And if we do not spend more time in listening than in talking to begin with, if we do not watch people's faces to see what is bringing peace and what is bringing anguish, it is certain that we will hurt others.

This does not mean that there are not times to bring anguish into community. It is sometimes important to bring people face to face with reality and remove the veil which is preventing anguish. But we must be there to see it through with them, and this is very different from hurting people unnecessarily by ill-placed jokes, lack of consideration and words which mean rejection.

I remember a young working girl at a retreat in Quebec. All the other members of the group had been quite well educated in theology; they spoke well, they used long words. They were all "wise and prudent". But they didn't realise that their conversation was just a mass of words for this very good little person, because no one spoke in a language that she could understand. All she felt was how uneducated and miserable and stupid she was.

We need to be sensitive to the needs of the people who live with us. This is where community will begin. It's important to know what will help them make the passage from the community for me to me for the community, to the outflowing of life which gives peace and love to those around us.

It will often be little things which persuade others that they are important to you — remembering a feast day, the anniversary of the death of a parent. There are a hundred and one small ways to convey sensitivity in any day. It can show in everything we do, from the way we serve the food and clean the floor to the way we arrange the flowers and knock at the door. Everything can be transformed from law into communion and gift, for a community begins with material things.

Food is important, and it should be good. Meals shouldn't be just something slopped onto the table; they should be times of communion. This is hard to convey in North America, where meals are often just something you throw into your stomach and have to get through. Certainly Canadians often find meals at l'Arche really long. And they are. But the meal is a whole ritual which begins with the soup and goes right through to the washing up. Washing up is an important time, because people work together, just as they share and communicate during the meal itself.

Meals are sharing, so it's important that the food should be shared too. Nowadays there's a tendency for everyone to have their own little pat of butter, their own little bottle of Coca-Cola, their own little packet of salt and pepper. One bottle for everyone to share may be less hygienic and less efficient, but it will bring more friendship. Even if you can find nothing else to say to someone, you can at least ask him for the salt, and this is the beginning of communication.

Meals shouldn't be serious times. They are times for laughter, because laughter opens people up, and a group which laughs is a group which is relaxed. And when people are relaxed, they can begin to grow together. Relaxation is like good soil, in which love can begin to grow. Nothing grows in hard soil. This is why it is important to have good food and good wine — in France at least. You may have people who squabble over the liturgy or theological problems, but at least let them relax over the food and wine and avoid ulcers!

Try to play stupid games — any sort. Let us come like children, to laugh and enjoy ourselves. This is what a community should learn to do — to relax and to welcome people. And as it grows, it learns to know people, with their needs, their hopes and their aspirations. Then it begins to accept, not judging or wanting people other than they are, but gradually discovering the music of their beings.

In Mother Teresa's chapel in Calcutta, you can hardly hear the priest because of the noise of the trams. But she and her sisters have gradually learned to love the trams, because they are part of humanity.

Humanity is not an ideal group of people living together. It is you and me and all of us, with our faults and our qualities, learning to accept, so that none of us is crushed by an ideal to which we cannot live up.

> **Judge not, that you be not judged. For with the judgment you pronounce you will be judged, and the measure you give will be the measure you get. Why do you see the speck that is in your brother's eye, but do not notice the log that is in your own eye?**
>
> **Or how can you say to your brother, "Let me take the speck out of your eye," when there is a log in your own eye? You hypocrite, first take the log out of your own eye, and then you will see clearly to take the speck out of your brother's eye.**
>
> **Matthew 7, 1-5**

It can be hard in a community when law has taken over from people and the law is so hard that everyone feels inferior. It is only as we accept people that we ourselves can drop our barriers, because we don't have to pretend that we're intelligent or good or wise: everyone knows that we are just people, trying to grow together.

One day a professor from the Sorbonne came to dinner with us, and we were trying to guess the population of a certain French town. Everyone threw in an idea — from fifty million people to five hundred. The professor guessed too. He was terribly embarrassed because he *had* to be right: so he asked what year we wanted the population for, and discussed the movement of industry and so on, for five whole minutes. And in the end he didn't win. But he couldn't bear the thought of losing to all these people who were mentally handicapped — he, a professor of the Sorbonne!

But if you don't know, you don't know. All you have to do is to say so. This can be hard for Superiors, who can feel they have to know every last detail of the will of God and everything else as well. Yet they are people too, and they can be wrong like anyone else. They should be able to say they don't know what to do, or that they were wrong, but that with God's grace they will know better and do better tomorrow.

If making a mistake diminishes authority, then something is wrong. It means the other members of the community are pushing the person with responsibility to a position where he must always be right, which is impossible. We must just be children of God together, in all our poverty and with all our ignorance and capacities. And when the barriers start to fall, this is the birth of mutual confidence, the end of fear, the beginning of trust in the actions of God, in each one. This is to live for the Saviour, the one who gives life.

And as the barriers fall, you begin to get the feeling of

84

unity, which is the reality of people growing together in love, sharing deeply and without fear. We do not have to hide our weaknesses or pretend we are better or wiser than others. We know we are accepted and loved. This brings peace, warmth, a relaxation of the whole being, and the spontaneous joy of being together. We live then not for ourselves, but for the glory of the Father, for the joy of the Father, for the wounded whom we welcome into our community. For this is community — bringing in wounded people who need the therapy of love, of peace, and of joy to heal their wounds and to call them to greater love.

But it is only, finally, by the Spirit coming into us that we can enter real community, whether this is a group of people who meet occasionally to pray or to share together, or people who live together. It is only when the Spirit changes our hearts that we can love all those of our community, whatever their age and background and character, because Jesus has called us to be together, because the other person is the gift of God to me today. This is the beauty of people when they live together, love together, when they are beginning to grow and share and be open in the Spirit together.

This is the beauty of mankind. This is something the goldfish never have and the cows in their field know nothing about. This is the beauty of mankind, when the Spirit of God has taken hold of the hearts of brothers and sisters and transformed them from hearts of stone to hearts of flesh. And they live then in the unity of love and commitment.

> That they may all be one; even as Thou, Father, art in me, and I in thee, that they also may be in us, so that the world may believe that thou hast sent me. The glory which thou hast given me I have given to them, that they may be one even as we are one, I in them and thou in me, that they may become perfectly one, so that the world

85

may know that thou hast sent me and hast loved them even as thou hast loved me.

John 17, 21-23

7

Love Your Neighbour

But the young lawyer, desiring to justify himself, said to Jesus: "And who is my neighbour?" Jesus replied, "A man was going down from Jerusalem to Jericho, and he fell among robbers, who stripped him and beat him, and departed, leaving him half dead. Now by chance a priest was going down that road; and when he saw him he passed by on the other side. So likewise a Levite, when he came to the place and saw him, passed by on the other side. But a Samaritan, as he journeyed, came to where he was; and when he saw him, he had compassion, and went to him and bound up his wounds, pouring on oil and wine; then he set him on his own beast and brought him to an inn, and took care of him. And the next day he took out two denarii and gave them to the innkeeper, saying, 'Take care of him; and whatever more you spend, I will repay you when I come back.' Which of these three, do you think, proved neighbour to the man who fell among the robbers?" He said, "The one who showed mercy on him." And Jesus said to him, "Go and do likewise."

Luke 10, 29-37

Most of us, if someone asked us who our neighbour was, would say he was the person living or sitting next to us. Jesus' reply to the young scribe is strange; he doesn't answer the question directly. He doesn't say, 'Your neighbour is the one close to you," for in a way this is obvious and natural. But he opens up new perspectives which do not seem evident. All men are my brothers and especially the wounded person whose path I cross.

Why didn't the priest and the Levite stop?

They had appointments in Jericho. They were busy people. They had to get to their meetings on time, which were every bit as important to them as ours are to us. Many of us are busy people too; we give classes and run home to cook for the people coming to dinner. We rarely have time for the essential; our lives can go by without living. We're so busy planning, organising, that when we find the man lying on the ground, we just haven't got time for him.

What we have to ask ourselves, we busy people, is whether our business is a flight from people. Is it something we do because we don't want to meet people, because we're frightened of them, of being disturbed by the unexpected, through which God often manifests himself?

Our business can be, and often is, a flight from compassion.

There are two sorts of needs that demand a response. It's very easy to lend someone money or drive them to a nearby city. It's a very limited demand; it has a beginning and an end.

What is much more disturbing is the second kind of demand. People ask you for food and you give it them, but they're going to be hungry again in five hours. If only there was a magic pill which meant they didn't have to get hungry again today, and tomorrow and the next day! This sort of request means unlimited meetings, because you don't know

where it's going to lead.

If you're in Howrah Station in Calcutta and you give a rupee to the first child who cries for it, then a hundred of them come, like bees round a honeypot, all crying, "Rupee, rupee!" If you're not careful, there will be a thousand, all crying, "Rupee, rupee!" So you have to be careful or you will close your heart, for this is unlimited, unending.

You decide to visit a prison once a month. But then you begin to listen to the wounded man, to sense his suffering; you hear about his wife and children, you begin to get involved, you come once a week instead of once a month. And then he comes out of prison and wants to come and see you. Maybe that's not quite what you thought the rules of the game were, but it's logical: you have gone to visit him and that means something to him; it has created something in his heart. So it is right and normal and just that he should come to see you. This can become embarassing and difficult. You become frightened.

Once a group of us — a priest, three sisters and some others — met with some people in one of the women's prisons in Cleveland; I think we had a good sharing. And the group of us said to each other afterwards: "We are prepared to visit these women in prison, because it's safe there, we are protected by guards. But soon they will be released and will go back to the inner city. Will we be ready to go and visit them there?" Yet if you've created a friendship in prison, you have to continue it where the people live, even if it's in a broken-down area where white people don't often go. That is part of shepherdhood. It's dangerous to create links and then drop them as if people don't exist any more.

In the meetings of people, there is something that has no end and we do not know where it will take us.

I remember talking with an American in London who had met a Jamaican who had just been put out of his house.

They exchanged addresses, and three weeks later the Jamaican turned up on the doorstep with all his suitcases. The link had been created. And all of us are more or less confronted with situations like this, where we cannot see what is going to happen. You visit a sick person and he asks when you are coming back. You talk to someone who is depressed and you sense that it's not going to stop there, that if you ring him he'll ring you back tonight, or tomorrow. So many wounded people need a shepherd, a friend, a brother, a comforter, someone to help them, to listen to them. We sense this as we get close to people and their needs. We then throw up barriers. What will happen to us, to our way of life, to our children, our family, the commitments we already have? We begin to sense that we won't be able to respond.

Why didn't the priest and the Levite stop?

Sometimes this natural defence is a realistic and healthy one. We have our commitments, we have our children, we may have frail health ourselves: we are obliged to say no.

But we must become conscious of the kind of barrier we are creating through this natural reaction. Who and what are we defending? Most of us are defending, more or less, a way of life, a whole style of living. We are living in a Rice Krispies civilization, where there is a set pattern for breakfast, for the type of house, of car and of holiday, for what will earn the neighbour's respect. The children are oriented to a particular form of existence that is usually called success. That doesn't mean following the Spirit; it means, for most parents, having a good job that brings in a comfortable living, getting married, and carrying on the North American way of life.

> Do not lay up for yourselves treasures on earth, where moth and rust consume and where thieves break in and steal, but lay up for yourselves treasures in heaven, where neither moth nor rust consumes and where

**thieves do not break in and steal. For where
your treasure is, there will your heart be
also.**

Why do we defend this way of life? If we delve into
ourselves, we will find that we are more anchored in the
values of our society than in those of the Gospel. Most or all
of us are closer to a Canadian who is not a Christian than to
our Indian or African brother who is. We react more
spontaneously to share with the North American, and this
means that we are more attached to our North American
way of life than to the culture of the Beatitudes.

So we create defences to protect our way of life. Anyone
who comes to upset it is a danger, because he is going to
make us give up our life style, and we don't want to leave
the television programmes that interest us, the books we
enjoy, the meals that make us happy.

Our way of life also corresponds in some way to our
function. Whether we are a priest, a bank manager or a
school teacher, we each have a place in society with a type
of house that is conventional and right, not only what we
want but what the people around want for us. Civilization
has given us our styles of life. In Quebec last year, they had
a problem in a new parish. The parishioners wanted the
most beautiful parsonage possible for their priest, the most
luxurious parsonage in Quebec. Their thought was kind, but
completely misguided; think of the priest trying to defend a
style of life that he didn't want himself but that people had
forced upon him.

Why didn't the priest and the Levite stop?

I remember a young couple, a social worker and a medical
student, who wanted to leave their apartment in one of the
richer parts of town and go and live with the little, wounded
people in a poorer section. Their friends told them to be
prudent, to think of the children: even though they didn't

have any yet; it would be bad for them when they arrived. (It's always bad for the children, unless it means spoiling them and giving them things and money.)

What their friends were saying was don't do it, because if you do, you're a threat to us. They weren't saying, "Do what you feel is right, be free!" The only thing you can say in this sort of situation is: "Are you doing it freely, or are you being influenced by some ideal which is more in your head than in your guts? If it's in your guts, then it's part of your being and you must do it. Go ahead, I'll help you. I'm not called to do it myself because of my particular situation, and I have to wait. But I love you for doing it."

Often friends have not the freedom to say this. They feel judged because someone is moving at a different pace; they haven't the freedom to let people evolve according to the Spirit. They tell them to be careful about enthusiasm, exaltation, delusion and so on. I imagine that many of the friends of Peter, John and James told them not to go too quickly, that they had a few reservations about some of the things this man Jesus was saying, that there were some really nice girls they could settle down with and a good living to make in the family fishing business. We worry about delusions, but we don't question the illusion of comfort, the illusions of our so-called friends or of North American civilization.

Parents are understandably worried when their child gets into drugs. But they are equally worried when their child gets into prayer groups, particularly if these are a bit charismatic! Many parents counsel their children to be really careful in following Jesus; they are rarely open to their child's call, unless the child is going into the priesthood in the traditional way, with chances of promotion to bishophood. Parents are always worrying about the security of the future, yet the dollar can inflate or deflate any day, and then we're all down to the same thing — growing potatoes. What they should do is to encourage the workings of the Spirit, believe and trust the child.

This doesn't mean that they should follow the child's simplest desires, his wishes and his fancies. The child will be called to something different from the parents, and the parents frequently feel this as a threat, if, for instance, the child wants to live poorly and they do not. We're easily threatened and frightened and so we put up barriers to protect our way of doing things, our consciousness of ourselves as men of power and capacity. The more we lack interior liberty, the more we have to amass wealth, the more we have to feel virtuous, capable of following an established rule. But these things are not important. What is important is to grow in liberty, in freedom to meet people, to welcome them, to discern where we can respond, to learn to look at people without fear, to learn to stop by a wounded person.

Why didn't the priest and the Levite stop? The wounded man, the man lying on the road between Jerusalem and Jericho is a threat. If they stop, what will happen to them?

The good Samaritan asks what will happen to the wounded man if he does not stop.

When we follow Jesus He says "Come", not come to Winnipeg or Florida, or something concrete that we can get our teeth into, but "Come and see." This is what He said to James and Andrew when He first met them.

> The next day again John was standing with two of his disciples; and he looked at Jesus as he walked, and said, "Behold the Lamb of God!" The two disciples heard him say this, and they followed Jesus. Jesus turned, and saw them following, and said to them, "What do you seek?" And they said to him, "Rabbi" (which means Teacher), "where are you staying?" He said to them, "Come and see."
>
> John 1, 35-39

In following Jesus, we come and see.

When we open ourselves to wounded people, it will be "come and see", for we don't know where they are leading us either.

Some stop.

But they refuse to look. That is the next step, to look someone in the eye without fear. Some people give money. Some came to L'Arche and talk of our devotion to our "little wounded ones". What they are saying is that to live with people like Raphael you have to be really special, because such people are no good. That is the worst insult possible, though they don't mean it. They don't realize what they are saying.

Or they try to put us on a pedestal! They tell us how much they admire us. Beware of admiration, for it is a cop-out. We are all called to the same reality, which is nothing but listening, understanding, loving.

Or they give us things. You can give things and hurt people; we must be careful what we give, that we don't use our gift in order to feel superior. Some people bring broken televisions, when in fact handicapped people need better televisions than other people, because of hearing and sight problems. Or they bring candies for "my children", some of whom are older than I am. They do not want their gifts to hurt anyone, but it is a sign of a lack of delicacy. You should not give unless you look and listen, and then the gift becomes a communion, a relationship, an understanding.

Some stop and look. Just that.

There are the professionals who come to L'Arche as if it was a zoo, to see a bunch of problems. They want to talk about the sexual problems of the people who live with us. Or people like the lady who came in to where a group of us were sitting round the table together, talking. She asked

"And what are you doing?" in the sort of voice that meant "And what are you teaching your children today?" I said to Raphael, who doesn't talk much, "So how's mathematics?" And he said "Merde!" I think he said what was in all our minds.

Once I was in a prison, talking to two or three hundred men there. At the end of the talk a man jumped up and started yelling at me, in language that even I didn't understand after eight years in the navy. What he was saying was: "You don't know what you're talking about. You haven't suffered like we have." He was really very tense, very loud, very violent. He said: "You don't know the suffering we have gone through, the wounds we have." And he told how he had seen his mother raped when he was seven, how he had been sold for homosexuality when he was ten, so that his father could drink. Afterwards, I went to talk with him, and he told me about his wife in a wheelchair.

Some stop, and look and then preach.

The word can become a barrier. An alcholic is told he must stop drinking; it's bad for his health. But he doesn't need to be told that — he's been vomiting all day. He doesn't need someone to proclaim the law to him, for he knows the law. What he wants is to find someone who will give him the force, the motivation, the thirst for life. It is not because you tell someone not to steal that he will not do it. He needs strength, he needs to be attached to someone who will give him the life and courage, the peace and love, which will help him not to steal, or not to take drugs, or not to drink, or not to fall into depression.

Or you can stop and look and then listen.

Listening means not just knowing the spoken language, but the meaning of words and actions. When a child steals, he is not just taking money; there is some reason. When a child gets into a temper, there is a reason. We must understand why someone is silent, we must understand their needs. We must listen not just with our ears, but with our whole body, through the eyes, the ears, the whole person, and try to understand.

We're not here to tell people what they need but to listen.

This is a civilization that wants to organize people and tell them what they should have. Certainly we must organize, but the first thing to organize is a place where people can meet and tell *their* needs; we are their servants to listen to them and to help fulfill these needs. In the only women's prison in Canada, at Kingston, some four years ago, there were a number of women from French Canada, yet not one guard, not one doctor or dentist, spoke French. It was only after I had spoken to the women in English that I was told that many did not understand me. It wasn't until 1972 that the French-speaking women were moved to part of one of the provincial prisons. But it would have been so simple just to have some guards who spoke French. That's all, just the recognition. When I spoke to these women in their own language, I saw the sufferings that were there because they felt despised, because they did not know how to express themselves. We do not mean to be contemptuous when we do not trouble to learn the other's language, when we get impatient because they do not understand ours too well; but it is another example of our lack of delicacy.

Furthermore, it is not simply a question of words. Frequently people will say all sorts of things that do not really express their needs. That is why, when we are confronted with deeply wounded people, we need experience, knowledge and understanding and discernment of the Spirit. When the beggar asks for money, he is asking for recognition. I remember a woman in Poland, begging outside a church. Our group had no Polish money, but one person knelt down and took her hands. Her face lit up, because that is what she was looking for: she was recognized as a person to be loved, not just a bucket into which we dump our bad consciences.

It is when you listen to people that you recognize them as having the right to speak, the right to express themselves. If you cut them off, you are telling them that they are not interesting, not worth listening to. And it is that which is fundamentally harmful to the wounded person.

We have to meet the wounded person with great respect, not trying to bring him up to where we think we are, not trying to make him respectable, but making him realise that we respect him as he is with the movement of his being and his capacity to grow.

There is beauty in Father Laborde, who lives in Calcutta with 52,000 people in an area of about 700 yards by 500 yards. It would have been easy for him to get thousands of dollars to build a nice school and oblige the children to come to it. But he didn't want any more money than was needed to help the people build their own community. It took much longer, but he got the people involved, so that they became men and women of dignity.

This is what a parent does for a child. He wants the child to find liberty, and it is the same for wounded people. It is not a question of doing things for them, but of giving them the chance to do things for themselves and others, of learning to do beautiful things. It will take longer to converse, to share, to get together, and maybe they won't do things our way. But they'll do them better; they'll do them in their own way.

In Canada, we have been going to the Eskimos and Indians and telling them what to do to have the good Canadian life, just as Europeans or North Americans who lived in India used to try to impose their own way of life on the people of that country. Yet by doing this we are condemning their culture, their parents and grandparents. We can crush a culture and create deep resentment in the hearts of those who have been crushed. Sometimes we have baptised the babies as if they were coming out of a machine, chalking up the numbers. And all we have done is to hurt thousands of people, by bringing them not to a belief in Jesus but to the imposition of a whole way of life, a culture which wounded them deeply because it looked down on them. It will take a long time before those we have wounded will recover, but we do not even realize that we have murdered people, the dynamism of their culture, the beauty of their creativity. We think we have done good things. We're blinded by our egoism and by our own desires for prestige and power and riches. We're worried all the time about what people think of us. We do not respect the Indian or the black man from the south of the United States who have different cultures from ours. We want to impose on them the culture of white people.

Yet we are a tiny, tiny group in this large world of ours. We do not constitute the majority of mankind. We are just a little group. We have the armaments, we have the power, we have the money to dole out, which makes us feel we are the liberators of the world. What we should do is to help others discover their culture, their strength and all in them which may be different to us but which is beautiful. We should learn to look with wonderment at the culture of another, the growth of another, the music of his being. We should learn to listen, to admire, to wonder, to call them forth, to help them create according to their own creativity and beauty.

An Indian once said to me: "You in the West have all the opportunities, the money, the education, the power, but you have lost the essential, the meaning of life."

> But if anyone has the world's goods and sees his brother in need, yet closes his heart against him, how does God's love abide in him?
>
> I John 3, 17

The love of God is a universal love which despises no man, for Jesus died for all people, all are his brothers. If we refuse to open ourselves up to a group of people because of their colour, because of their background, because of their education, because of sickness at birth, then the love of God does not abide in us.

Very soon, a people who do not open themselves up to all people, to wounded people, to little people, will lose the sense of prayer, because the love of God is not in their hearts. They will no longer pray.

But those who go forth to wounded ones in a spirit of welcome, whatever religious label is round their necks, will have hearts that gradually open to this love of God. As long as we are going out to people of other cultures, we must go not to do good, but to listen, to touch, to admire, to watch them grow in the beauty of their being, to see them flower in their own language, to discover the diversity of mankind.

A garden full of nothing but lilies would be a bit boring.

This means that in many ways we must forget ourselves. It does not mean that we must renounce our own culture. We must put aside certain aspects of our being which make us think that our culture is the best and should be imposed on all. We must discover the relativity of our own way of life, the beauty of the nomad, the tuarag in Southern Algeria, the gypsy, the Bengali, the distinctiveness of each one. Just because some men are nomads, doesn't mean that a sedentary life is to be condemned. I can live my life, but I must open myself to the other and his ways, as he will gradually become confident enough to open to mine. Gradually it will be through the meeting of peoples that the salvation of mankind will come, as the west begins to understand the culture of the east and the east the culture of the west. But it is not just mutual understanding that is important. The disciple of Jesus has a deep thirst to communicate to the wounded person not just a human hope, but much more, the Spirit of Jesus, the peace of Jesus, the Beatitudes. He knows that salvation can only come through real love and compassion, through a rebirth in the Spirit.

But he cannot impose or force the message of love. All he can do perhaps is to revive in the heart of the wounded person a desire for this love and peace. By his very presence, silent and compassionate, the disciple of Jesus becomes a presence of Jesus to the wounded. "It is no longer I that live but Christ who lives in me." (Galatians 2, 20) Through this love and compassion the wounded person can discover that he is loved by his God.

One has to begin with wounded people *by living with them.* In this time, when we are aiming to become more and more professionalised, we tend to forget that the basis of life is mutual confidence, mutual respect, deep love and acceptance. Once people have this, they can begin to grow with the professional help they need. Often they cannot find people who will live with them — and that does not necessarily mean to occupy the same house. It means to be open, to understand, to share, not to impose but to grow together, in free expression and in liberty, in positive love.

Where is the love?

There was a very beautiful girl in a Canadian hospital, about seventeen or eighteen, in a ward with about forty others, some quite handicapped and disturbed. There were no toys, no games. They were just sitting. The doors, of course, were locked. Anne had a very beautiful face. I asked how long it was since she had been home? She didn't answer. Had she been at Christmas? No. She hadn't been home for a long, long time. She told me home was sixty miles away. Actually, it was in the same city, but the people in the hospital didn't dare tell her. There was great beauty in her face, no deep hatred. There was just depression or sadness. She didn't, in a way, have the strength to hate.

Frequently children who have been hurt like that turn their hatred upon themselves and commit various forms of suicide. They refuse to live. They can commit suicide by creating the barriers we call psychoses; they hide themselves away from the reality that hurts, so that no relationship with people is possible.

There was a girl in one of the large asylums in Paris, strapped to her bed, because otherwise she would scratch her face and eyes. The doctor said it was partly his fault that she was like this. Three years ago, she came to the hospital; she had to be spoon-fed, she did not move her eyes, she did not react to words. The only thing she reacted to was food — if she liked it she would smile, if not she would vomit. The doctor decided to try to reach her. He spent a lot of time with the girl. He fed her, he touched her, linking her relationship with food to a person, himself. This is the way children begin life, by food and touch in the arms of the mother, gradually moving on to other realities, like a toy, or other people. So this girl, at the age of fourteen or so, opened to reality, but reality for a girl like this is not a toy or the table or the bed, but a person. And so the doctor became everything to her, became her all.

And then, he stopped seeing her. He had completed his experiment. From that moment, she tried to commit suicide in a violent way. She had probably been deeply hurt when she was a tiny child, and she had closed herself off from reality, which was hell. For the weakness of a child demands a relationship with a person who can understand his delicacy and weakness. If he is treated with harshness and rejection, he will close himself off from a world that hates him. This is what the girl did until the doctor drew her forth and she came to trust him. And then she was dropped. She knew she was no good, that she was evil, that she was not wanted. So she went into a more violent form of suicide and she will stay that way, with her hands bandaged to her bed. She will certainly not succumb to the temptation of meeting someone again.

It is dangerous to meet people who do not really love.

If people have been deeply hurt and looked upon as inferior, their wounds say: "I am no good, I am evil. Nobody wants to love me. Nobody will love me."

A child who has experienced this becomes aggressive and violent. He has to destroy the hell that is around him. This is the world of delinquents, the young people who fill our reform schools, full of hate because no one has ever said, "You're worthwhile, you are lovable, you have something beautiful inside you which must flower."

This is often the reason that people go into alcoholism or drug addiction, or forms of violence, because there is a deep void in their being which they cannot fill up. They are continually looking for a reality to fill them up. This is the yearning for love.

> **Come to me, all who labour and are heavy laden, and I will give you rest. Take my yoke upon you, and learn from me; for I am gentle and lowly in heart, and you will find rest for your souls. For my yoke is easy and my burden is light.**
>
> **Matthew 11, 28-30**

To meet Jesus in the wounded demands that we come with deep respect. It is not enough to go to them through a sense of duty, just because God told us to visit the poor. We must really love them.

Look. Listen. Touch. Touch the wounded person, touch his hand, make him realize we are close. The Spirit leads us from stopping to looking, to listening and then to touching, as he draws us from our culture, our style of life, our pattern of thinking, the emphasis on particular forms and types of education. He gradually breaks all these down, and allows us to listen to and look at people without fear.

This does not mean that tomorrow we start to throw our arms round people of other cultures. It doesn't work like that. To begin with, we should get down on our knees and ask the forgiveness of our wounded brothers, who today are still in hospitals, shut up because they were handicapped as

102

children. Ask pardon of those who we have shut up behind prison bars because, in many ways, it is our attitudes that have pushed them there and keep them there. We send them back when we do not welcome them at the end of their time. Ask forgiveness of our own Canadian Indians. Ask for the pardon of God.

But asking pardon is already a commitment to listen, to understand. We must listen quietly, not rushing at people, for their wounds are too great. We must just wait and let the growth happen, slowly listening to each other and becoming committed to each other. And then we begin to live together.

So we will begin to open half-way houses for men coming out of prison, or to bring into our homes people who have spent many years in hospitals for the handicapped, or to go and share with people in the poor parts of the city. We won't feel triumphant, but humble and repentant. We will just listen quietly and gently, in no way feeling that we are better, rather feeling deep grief in our own being for the responsibility we carry personally and collectively as a nation and so-called disciples of Jesus. We cannot take in every person and look after everyone. When Peter and John stood in front of the lame beggar and the beggar cried out for money, Peter said, "I have no silver and gold, but I give you what I have; in the name of Jesus Christ of Nazareth, walk." (Acts 3, 6)

Maybe all we can say is "I have no money, I have little time. But I give you my peace. And I love you. I cannot stay with you, but I want you to know I believe in you. I believe you can do beautiful things. I believe that Jesus loves you. I believe that you can grow as a child of God, filled with the Spirit. It will take time, but be confident, trust Him, hope in Him and rise up on the path of life."

This is the meeting that should take place, as the Spirit breaks down the barriers of our being, our style of life and culture, as He brings us close to people. In the Spirit, hidden in the heart of Jesus, we become healers of men, giving them confidence and hope that the world is not hell but a place where we learn to prepare for Paradise, for the Wedding where we are all guests, and so we will become real instruments of Jesus and his love. We will give Jesus, who alone heals the wounds of humanity.

> **Which of these three, do you think, proved neighbour to the man who fell among the robbers? The young lawyer said, "The one who showed mercy on him." And Jesus said to him, "Go and do likewise."**
>
> **Luke 10, 36-37**

8

Abide in My Love

Sometimes the good news, the Gospel itself, seems nothing more than a dream — very beautiful, but still a dream. The Beatitudes can sound just fine, the idea of living like the birds of heaven or the flowers of the field is very poetic, the idea of loving our enemy, loving as Jesus loves, is very admirable. But they are totally impractical. They are an impossible dream.

As we look through history, as we look at the problems of the world today, we tend to become discouraged. The dream of Jesus seems impossible for modern man. There doesn't seem to be much place for the Gospels in a world overwhelmed with problems of pollution, population, poverty and drought, in a world delving into space and into the depths of man's psychology, in a world of needs which range from water itself to refrigerators and cars. The Gospels are fine poetry, but the reality of our world is the cities with eight million people and all the problems these bring; reality is the muggings and the crime and the man from whom we must protect ourselves by building prisons, whatever we may say about the need to reform the penal system.

Yet Jesus is calling us to the Beatitudes, to love of our enemies and to poverty. And there are moments when we can sense that if this world is to continue at all, there must be a transformation of men's hearts. As we go forward into history with all the continuing aggression and war and anguish, we can be at least perplexed if not anguished for tomorrow.

And then we think of the little old woman in Cleveland who said: "I've been walking with him for forty years." And of Jean-Claude telling us about Jesus at Lourdes. And of Mark, who died of leukemia when he was sixteen, who after having been apparently cured (though losing his hearing and his hair because of the drugs he had taken), learned again that he had only weeks to live. "Now and again," he said, "I lose peace." He said it in a way that meant that pretty well all the time he had peace. He was very, very close to Jesus.

Or we think of Joan, who organized the French part of the pilgrimage that brought our handicapped brothers and sisters from around the world to Lourdes. She and her husband had two very severely handicapped children; they loved each other deeply. Suddenly, when she was in Paris, she heard that her husband, a handsome farmer who had been perfectly well until then, had fallen ill. By the time she arrived home, he had already died of a heart attack. She knelt by his bed and said: "God gave him to me, God has taken him back." When we had taken him home and dressed him and prepared the room, Joan just said, "Let's sing the Magnificat together."

So, as we look through the world and the political and economic movements in which it seems to be caught up, we find that God is present after all. His presence is a reality in wounded people, in little people, in people doing things that alone they would be unable to do. We begin to see that God is master of the impossible and that he is transforming the hearts of people. We begin to see that the dream of Jesus does come true, in the hearts of little people. This is a fundamental reality. When you have occasion to listen to people — at retreats for example — they tell you how God acts in their hearts, how the call comes to them, how the transformation takes place. It is always unique and different for each one, and yet, there is something similar in

106

the way God acts in the hearts of each one of us.

> **Jesus looked at them and said, "With men it is impossible, but not with God; for all things are possible with God."**
>
> **Mark 10, 27**

We begin to sense our poverty when we begin to sense how far away we are from the Master of the Beatitudes, when we begin to sense how little we love our enemies, how aggressive we are, how little we are good shepherds, how little we really live in community, how little we strive to bridge the division and disunity of this world. We begin to sense that we need to be healed and to be transformed, because God is calling us to something that we cannot possibly do by ourselves. We cannot love an enemy: we flee from an enemy, we are aggressive towards him, we hurt and wound him. We disregard little people. We're frightened. When we begin to sense all the security we have in our lives that prevents us opening ourselves to the Spirit, when we sense how comfortable we are, how we seek comfort rather than compassion and love — then we are preparing the road to transformation.

We have to be careful during a retreat. We can listen to the music of the word of Jesus and tell ourselves how nice these thoughts are. We can enjoy the company and the food and the talks; we can have a nice spiritual holiday. But we must beware of this holiday, for today in the slums, in the prisons, in hospitals throughout the world, people are sweating it out. If our dream does not become a determination, an action, a yearning, then we can deeply damage ourselves and our brothers and sisters.

The word of Jesus demands action, which means not just doing things, but a certain response to a call. It means a "yes" and we have to be vigilant to see what that "yes" means. God will not be mocked. To play with his things is literally to play with fire, for He is a living, loving person and He does not want spectators basking in the sun. The reality of the Gospels is a true reality, and God's call is a real call, His desire a real desire. It is important that each of us respond as the Spirit wants us to respond.

The "yes" will be an entering into the paths of prayer, which is not just a mumbling of words, or even necessarily the experience of a charismatic movement, but union with God, union with Jesus. It is the opening up of our being to love, to the Spirit coming into us, the taking of our being into its very depths, uniting us to Jesus, in silent loving prayer. This prayer will draw us to a deep compassion for all, but especially for wounded people. It means entering into the silent abidings of love, for Jesus speaks to us in the deep silence of our being and He speaks to us in quiet contemplation. Certainly He can and does awaken charismatic gifts in many people and this is good; but at the same time these gifts are only a tiny aspect of His vast gifts of love and of peace in deep union.

> **You are already made clean by the word which I have spoken to you. Abide in me and I in you. As the branch cannot bear fruit by itself, unless it abides in the vine, neither can you, unless you abide in me. I am the vine, you are the branches. He who abides in me and I in him, he it is that bears much fruit, for apart from me you can do nothing. If a man does not abide in me, he is cast forth as a branch and withers; and the branches are gathered, thrown into the fire and burned.**
>
> **John 15, 3-6**

Jesus often uses the word "abide". To abide in Jesus is what prayer is about. We must live this word and open up the chalice of our being to the presence of God, enter into His silence. We must learn to rest in that peace which comes when He touches our hearts. We must know that this peace is the presence of God, that this is how God speaks to us — through this love which touches us at our core and flows through all our being and plunges us into silence. We must be open to this peace.

> As the Father has loved me, so have I loved you; abide in my love. If you keep my commandments, you will abide in my love, just as I have kept my Father's commandments and abide in his love. These things I have spoken to you, that my joy may be in you, and that your joy may be full.
>
> John 15, 9-11

The healing and transforming process is begun and completed in this abiding in Jesus in prayer. It is to the extent that we abide in him that we are gradually transformed, and discover that our enemies cease to be enemies, and that we can love them. It is to the extent that we abide in Jesus that we can become a peacemaker and thus a child of God.

> Blessed are the peace makers, for they shall be called sons of God.
>
> Matthew 5, 9

The peace maker is the one who gives the peace of Jesus, who reconciles and unites divided people. We can become this man of peace through and in the Spirit. We cannot do it by ourselves, but if we abide, if we really enter into the Beatitudes, then it becomes possible.

We know we cannot do this by ourselves. This is why Jesus came; this is precisely why he sends his Spirit to us, to transform us. This is what Jesus repeats and repeats.

> If you love me, you will keep my command- ments. And I will pray the Father and he

will give you another Paraclete, to be with
you for ever, even the Spirit of Truth,
whom the world cannot receive, because it
neither sees him nor knows him; you know
him, for he dwells with you, and will be in
you.

John 14, 15-17

This is the Spirit that Jesus sends to us.

These things I have spoken to you, while I
am still with you. But the Paraclete, the
Holy Spirit, whom the Father will send in
my name, he will teach you all things, and
bring to your remembrance all that I have
said to you. Peace I leave with you; my
peace I give to you.

John 14, 25-27

But when the Paraclete comes, whom I shall
send to you from the Father, even the Spirit
of truth, who proceeds from the Father, he
will bear witness to me; and you also are
witnesses, because you have been with me
from the beginning.

John 15, 26-27

Jesus came to send us his Spirit and to transform our
hearts of stone into hearts of flesh. This is the promise that
he made to us through our fathers:

I will sprinkle clean water upon you, and
you will be clean from all your
uncleannesses, and from all your idols I will
cleanse you. A new heart I will give you,
and a new spirit I will put within you; and I
will take out of your flesh the heart of stone
and give you a heart of flesh. And I will put

**my spirit within you, and cause you to walk
in my statutes and be careful to observe my
ordinances.**

Ezekiel 36, 25-27

This is the promise of God which permits us to do those things that we cannot do ourselves — to love as Jesus loves, to enter into the paths of the Beatitudes, to become poor and loving, to become gentle and peaceful, to become strong and to search for justice at all times. This is what the healing power of the Spirit is for, this power which transforms us and makes us real disciples of Jesus, followers of the Lamb and of the Shepherd. We begin to walk in his footsteps. He will give us the courage to look at tomorrow, to accept the present. He will give us the courage to forgive — for many of us bear the scars of resentment and have yet to learn to forgive, to love those who have hurt us, to attain interior freedom.

To enter into this healing process, we have to learn to be silent. It is very easy, after having heard the word of God, to go out and shout it. This can be a form of escape from letting the word of God penetrate those parts of our hearts where we may feel a certain guilt, a lack of faith and of generosity. We can quickly turn away from the reality of our being, instead of welcoming all our lack of faith, offering it to the Spirit, weeping and saying: "Have mercy on me, come and heal me and transform me."

This is why we need times of searching, of yearning, of quiet prayer. It is so good to have moments of real quiet, when we can enter a world of silence. And it is in this silence that the Spirit speaks to us, gives us the strength and the love to forgive the past and to accept its wounds. It is during these moments of silence that the seeds are sown in our hearts and this is why it is important that we take much more time to yearn for the Spirit to come into us.

Prayer may be hard at these times, for the world of transformation is not easy. We are so used to instant coffee,

111

instant tea and instant meals that we forget we have to work for things that are worthwhile. And nothing is more worthwhile than to be called to this land of liberty, this land of joy and peace, for which we are all yearning.

What is important is the growth of commitment and of love in a world where there is strife and death, where never before has there been such a need for real disciples of Jesus, real shepherds, real healers in the Spirit. To say "yes" to Jesus is a commitment, and then we use the means He gives us to walk with Him. We find our nourishment in prayer, in yearning, in reading and loving His word, in listening to and being committed to little and wounded people. Thus we become re-created by the Spirit and can go forth with greater determination, greater humility and greater love, more and more open to the call of the Beloved.

We must learn to be faithful in love, for love is not just some passing exaltation, some joyous moment. Love is fidelity to the loved one, learning to wait, to grow together. Love is the branch abiding in the vine. We must learn to be faithful, and fidelity means determination, holding on under criticism, under laughter, in the face of all the temptations that might surround us. We must learn fidelity to the Lover who is calling us forth to walk with Him in light and in peace. Love is not to be afraid.

9

Come Forth

As we become conscious of the depths of the call of Jesus, we become conscious also of our poverty and our sinfulness, of all we do not do because we are caught up in our selfishness. He comes close to us as He makes us conscious of our aggressions, our depressions, our cowardice, our bitterness: as we begin to sense the depths of our indifference, and of our fears. When we get close to our real poverty and so to a certain consciousness of death, then only can we begin to sense the nearness of rebirth and of the resurrection. And the resurrection is the calling forth of the Spirit inside me — God calling me forth from the grave of my own being.

The hand of the Lord was upon me, and he brought me out by the Spirit of the Lord, and set me down in the midst of the valley; it was full of bones. And he led me round among them; and behold, there were very many upon the valley; and lo, they were very dry. And he said to me, "Son of man, can these bones live?" And I answered, "O Lord God, thou knowest." Again he said to me, "Prophesy to these bones, and say to them, O dry bones, hear the word of the Lord. Thus says the Lord God to these bones: Behold, I will cause breath to enter you, and you shall live. And I will lay sinews upon you, and cover you with skin, and put

breath in you, and you shall live; and you shall know that I am the Lord."

So I prophesied as I was commanded; and as I prophesied, there was a noise, and behold a rattling; and the bones came together, bone to its bone. And as I looked, there were sinews on them, and flesh had come upon them, and skin had covered them; but there was no breath in them. Then he said to me, "Prophesy to the breath, prophesy, son of man, and say to the breath, Thus says the Lord God: Come from the four winds, O breath, and breathe upon these slain, that they may live. So I prophesied as he commanded me, and the breath came into them, and they lived, and stood upon their feet, an exceedingly great host.

Then he said to me, "Son of man, these bones are the whole house of Israel. Behold, they say, 'Our bones are dried up and our hope is lost; we are clean cut off.' "

Ezekiel 37, 1-11

These words still live. So many say they are all dried up inside. They have lost hope. They live with their depression, lack of openness. They say they are cut off from God — perhaps He doesn't even exist.

Many people today feel their bones are dried up. There is nothing that flows inside, just a void or confusion and darkness. There seems to be no hope, no way out of the political, economic and religious structures, no way to close the divisions of humanity. The only thing left is to flounder into a world of drugs or alcohol or sexuality. "Let's not think of others, let's just make money and do what we want." "There is no hope for mankind, we must look out for ourselves." This form of spiritual death is very common.

How quickly the life of the Spirit can become dried up

inside us. Some who have followed Jesus for many years can think back to the days when they were young and their hearts were filled with generosity and the desire to pray, to love Jesus. Now they hardly pray at all except in formulas and their generosities have turned to interior bickerings; they've lost light and hope. Many of us find ourselves all dried up inside, ten, twenty or thirty years after giving ourselves to Jesus. We either remain in the bleakness of our sadness or we seek compensation in the search for power or in internal dissentions and petty squabblings.

The same thing happens in marriage. So many enter into it with such beauty. Their hearts are open, filled with expectations and with love. Then gradually hearts harden and close, as the man becomes more involved with work and less tender, loving and understanding. Work becomes an escape and the wife, herself wounded, escapes into her children. She cuts herself off from her husband and becomes concerned only for the children and the cleanliness of the house. So gradually their unity, which was so beautiful at the start, begins to dry up as each tries to find what compensations he can. There is anguish and separation. The mother, instead of hoping that her children will reach greater and greater liberty, becomes more and more possessive as she senses that one day she will again be alone with her husband.

Young people may have had happiness in childhood, but as they grow up to longer hours of school and study, they develop a sense of worthlessness. They begin to judge their parents, cutting themselves off, feeling that they cannot live in the structures of our society.

The tendency for our bones to dry up, for our hope to be cut off, is very deep in all our hearts, whether we are young or old, married or in a consecrated state. We become hard, we begin to judge and condemn. We lose our openness and fluidity, we reject new ideas, we become cynical. We want to kill anything that seems alive, because the seeds of death have been planted in us and are beginning to grow.

The Spirit can only let us discover this darkness of our being when light is close by.

> Therefore prophesy, and say to them, Thus says the Lord God: Behold, I will open your graves, O my people; and I will bring you home into the land of Israel. And you shall know that I am the Lord, when I open your graves and raise you from your graves, O my people. And I will put my Spirit within you, and you shall live, and I will place you in your own land; then you shall know that I, the Lord, have spoken, and I have done it, says the Lord.
>
> **Ezekiel 37, 12-14**

> He said therefore, "What is the kingdom of God like? And to what shall I compare it? It is like a grain of mustard seed which a man took and sowed in his garden; and it grew and became a tree, and the birds of the air made nests in its branches."
>
> **Luke 13, 18-19**

As the seed of the Spirit is planted, there is a very quiet moment of peace. Jesus came to transform us, to give us this new Spirit, the Spirit of the Father. This is what He announced.

> I will not leave you desolate; I will come to you.
>
> **John 14, 18**

> But the Paraclete, the Holy Spirit whom the Father will send in my name, he will teach you all things, and bring to your remembrance all that I have said to you.
>
> **John 14, 26**

116

This is the manifestation of the Spirit in our being. It is this Spirit which will heal us of our fears and selfishness and teach us to love, with all the gentleness and commitment of a good shepherd. He will teach us to love those of other cultures, those whom our country has murdered in different ways, those in far-off lands. He will teach us to love them not by imposing our being on them, not by telling them how much they have to learn from us, but by calling forth their own creativity, their beauty, by calling them forth to love.

The Spirit cures our hearts, takes away bitterness and cynicism, and teaches us to love our enemies. As He continues to touch us, we begin to sense the beauty of the Kingdom of God — the Kingdom like a treasure hidden in a field, like a pearl of great price.

When we begin to sense this transformation of the Spirit, this quiet, this stillness, this hope, this peace, then we begin to realise that the possessions we have valued are a weight that we need to throw off. Things begin to mean less because now we have something else — peace and liberty, a stillness, a richness of heart.

> **Do not lay up for yourselves treasures on earth, where moth and rust consume and where thieves break in and steal, but lay up for yourselves treasures in heaven, where neither moth nor rust consumes and where thieves do not break in and steal. For where your treasure is, there will your heart be also.**
>
> **Matthew 6, 19-21**

Then we begin to understand what Jesus is talking about when he talks of poverty. We begin to understand that our treasure is in our hearts, in our communities whether this is our family or the community we are called to live with. Our treasure is in the heart, and we must get rid of anything that does not let our hearts flower, that does not let this inner part of our beings evolve, for it is in the inner heart that the Spirit resides.

> **Do you not know that you are God's temple and that God's Spirit dwells in you?**
> **I Corinthians 3, 16**

The Spirit begins to make us yearn for prayer, for communion with people. He gives us a desire to listen. He begins to take anguish and fear away from us.

But the Spirit is not only a giver. The Spirit is also an interior light and the movement of our lives is a growth. The life of the Spirit is not a big happening. It is a seed that must grow quietly and gently, and like any seed, it needs nourishment. One of the things the Spirit asks of us is to begin to sense what nourishment we need for this love within us to grow, because this seed is very fragile. It can quickly be stifled by weeds.

> **Hear then the parable of the sower. When any one hears the word of the kingdom and does not understand it, the evil one comes and snatches away what is sown in his heart; this is what was sown along the path. As for what was sown on rocky ground, this is he who hears the word and immediately receives it with joy; yet he has no root in himself, but endures for a while, and when tribulation or persecution arises on account of the word, immediately he falls away. As for what was sown among thorns, this is he who hears the word, but the cares of the world and the delight in riches choke the word, and it proves unfruitful.**
> **Matthew 13, 18-23**

So we must be careful as we gather this treasure, this

seed, into our beings. What must we separate ourselves from? What are the weeds that must be plucked out? What must we beware of? What is the nourishment we need for the Spirit to grow in us in all His gentleness?

We must become conscious that this treasure must not just be conserved or even less, squandered, but nourished. For it is not just for my life but also for the life of others. If we let the seed grow, it will bear much fruit, and this is the desire of Jesus.

> **I am the vine, you are the branches. He who abides in me and I in him, he it is that bears much fruit, for apart from me you can do nothing. By this my Father is glorified, that you bear much fruit, and so prove to be my disciples.**
>
> **John 15, 5, 8**

All of us are called forth, with this tiny seed of the Spirit, to grow and to nourish and to heal mankind. This is our responsibility: to go forth to all men. The fruit is not for us, for our joy and plenitude, but for mankind, for the people of God. We must gradually discover this power which has been given to us and is not ours: it is the Spirit and it is Jesus living in us.

It is not we who are called to do good, but the Spirit of God in us. He comes to live in us as in a temple and flows out from us to awaken the spirit in the hearts of others, so that they too may become conscious of the beauty of their temple, so that they may discover under all the bitterness and despair the presence of God living in them and waiting to be awakened. It is a responsibility to welcome the Spirit of Jesus into our being, just as Mary carried responsibility when she welcomed His physical presence into her womb.

The first thing to do as we become conscious that we are the temple of the Spirit is to give thanks, as Mary did when she sang the Magnificat:

> My soul magnifies the Lord, and my spirit
> rejoices in God my Saviour, for he has
> regarded the low estate of his handmaiden.
> For behold, henceforth all generations
> will call me blessed;
> for he who is mighty has done great things
> for me,
> and holy is his name.
>
> Luke 1, 46-49

Frequently when the Spirit comes into our being we discover his presence by its fruits. There are three of these fruits. The first is the *light* which is gradually taking the place of darkness, of confusion; light which is a hope, a dynamism, a force.

There are times when we sense the light within us, urging us forth to delight in truth, the truth in our own being, the truth of the word of God, of reality, of people. The light urges us to separate ourselves from anything which is not true, from all that is darkness, lies or illusion, for we sense that it is the truth which will set us free. We begin to love the universe, this extraordinary universe with the stars and the moon and the sun, the winds, the seasons, the lands, the animals and the people. We begin to look at the music and the suffering of the world. We begin to discover the beauty of the word of God and to love it. And thus gradually we begin to lose our heaviness and we begin to grow in hope. The wings of our being come forth. We begin to urge and to yearn. We are reborn in hope.

This is the light which grows in us, which urges us on to greater understanding of the beauties of people and of the universe and gradually calls us forth to wonderment and contemplation. We begin to look at this universe and at Jesus with the eyes of a child, with the peace, the excitement, the adoration of a child. This is the light as it grows in us: to love reality.

The second fruit of the Spirit as He comes into my being is to make me reject my aggressiveness and fear of people, teaching me *to love the enemy*, he who is a threat to me. He sets me free from the desire to hurt, to hide, to destroy, to criticize, to laugh at people instead of with them. Gradually the Spirit takes away all the powers of division that are in me and creates powers of understanding and reconciliation. He gradually makes me aware of the walls and the barriers in me, the fears, the bitterness, the refusal to speak with people or to forgive, the impatience and anger, and He liberates me to love. This is the work of the Spirit. We cannot do it by ourselves. We cannot change the darkness of our being into light, nor hatred into love.

Finally, He comes with *His peace*, which is in many ways the union of the light and the love, the death of aggressiveness and the birth of hope. This peace is not just an absence of war. It is nothing to do with my saying "leave me in peace" and shutting myself away. Peace is something which flows out from me. It is union with Jesus and with people. It was at the heart of the first Christian community where Jesus, Mary and Joseph lived. It is a sign of the unity of the Father and the Son and the Spirit. It was at the heart of the first Christian communities after the Spirit had come upon the twelve at Pentecost. It is the unity between people that goes beyond words. And as the Spirit of Jesus flows through them, it brings a closeness which is not a closing-off, but is a vast welcome for all men and especially the poor and the wounded, my brothers and sisters.

As we become conscious of the growth of light, of the death of aggressiveness and the birth of life, we must begin with our minds to see what this implies for our way of life. We must begin to see what will help the life of the Spirit to grow. Sometimes we will be confronted with difficult decisions between keeping contact with certain so-called friends who hold us back from God or being more with our brothers and sisters in the Spirit. We must choose and we must act. We must realize the gravity of the things of God. We cannot play around, wailing like spoilt children because God does not manifest Himself to us. We cannot say "Oh God, feed the hungry," when we are not doing it ourselves.

We have to be conscious of the way God operates in us. We must find friends in the Spirit who will urge us forward and encourage us, with whom we can pray, whom we can ring up and ask to pray for us when it is hard. They will warm us in times of despair and sadness, and we will be open to them when they come to us. We will encourage each other as brothers and sisters to be faithful.

We need each other to grow in love, to be faithful to the light and the Spirit which Jesus has given to us and which is our responsibility. We need the nourishment of prayer, of friendship. We need the nourishment of the body of Jesus, as we go forth and open ourselves to wounded people, to our enemies. We need the nourishment of God as we read the words of Jesus, the nourishment of our love for the vast community of the faithful, for the church, for all the followers of Jesus. We have to grow in this love and to desire that these people of God become truly that — humble, poor, beautiful, hungry and thirsty for justice.

We need to discover the nourishment and be determined to live by it. It might be meeting together to pray, perhaps in humble charismatic prayer, filled with the joy of the Spirit, and openness to others — not condemning or judging, but flowing from the Spirit in quiet healing. It might be calling forth into quiet, silent contemplative prayer, where there are no words, but a deepening of peace, abiding at the feet of Jesus and learning to pray as Mary prayed: the quiet contemplation of Charles de Foucauld or Teresa of Avila, which is at the heart of the tradition of the saints through the ages. It might be a prayer of peace, a prayer of repose, a prayer of great love which pulls us into long hours of just being possessed by the silence of God. It might be quiet recitation of the rosary, the peaceful naming of the word of God, the name of Jesus, the name of Mary, or just the quiet prayer of the liturgy, the reading of the psalms. There are all these forms of dialogue with our Father, with his Son and with the Spirit.

If we learn the nourishment, if we let our soil be tilled, the earth turned over by the sufferings that come through life, then gradually the Spirit grows in us and we begin to perceive the fruits. We begin to sense what it means to walk in the Spirit, to love in the Spirit, to live in the Spirit.

> **But those who live according to the Spirit set their minds on the things of the Spirit.**
> **Romans 8, 5**

> **But you are not in the flesh, you are in the Spirit, if in fact the Spirit of God dwells in you.**
> **Romans 8, 9**

> **For all who are led by the Spirit of God are sons of God. For you did not receive the spirit of slavery to fall back into fear, but you have received the spirit of sonship. When we cry "Abba! Father!" it is the Spirit himself bearing witness with our spirit that we are children of God, and if children, then heirs, heirs of God and fellow heirs with Christ, provided we suffer with him in order that we may also be glorified with him.**
> **Romans 8, 14-17**

Come to the Wedding Feast

10

The heart of man yearns to love and to be loved. We need not just to be admired, but to have somebody care deeply for us and to be able to care for him. There is a great thirst in our being to find the person who will really understand us, who will comfort us, who will need us, who will share with us.

Love is strange and beautiful; there are so many contradictions in it. It is in some mysterious way beyond time — a communion and a presence which is anchored in eternity. And yet it is firmly anchored in time, for if it is the opening of the gates of our being, it is also daily fidelity. It is mutual forgiveness, mutual help in times of suffering and difficulty. It is fidelity to people, with all the difficulty that this can bring when the first excitement is confronted with everyday reality.

Love is also a quest for the infinite. This is in a way the beauty but also the tragedy of man. We always want to go further and wider, higher and deeper — whether to the stars, or in knowledge, in possessions or an experience of the infinite. This is at the heart of mysticism in all civilizations and religions. We seek union with the infinite: it is this which is the source of many experiments with drugs or alcohol: it is this which is at the source of all human activity. This quest for the non-finite is the deep motivation in domination — to possess more and more power. So it is also in love. We wish to love in an infinite way, to love eternally, without limit and until death.

125

And yet we are very close to the earth. We are very limited by our need for food and sleep, by our capacity for fatigue and sickness. We are limited by our human bodies as we are limited in our minds and hearts. And it is this conflict between the limitations of our being — metaphysical as well as purely physical and spiritual — which brings much of the anguish of the human condition. We are made for the infinite, but we are so terribly finite.

In our thirst for love we very quickly idealise, wanting the loved one to be perfect. Although we soon discover that the perfect man and woman do not exist, yet the thirst for perfection, for the meeting which will carry us out of time into an embrace of eternity, is still there. And when man does not find this perfect love, he creates barriers. He will tend to conclude, as these barriers grow, that love does not exist.

This is the philosophy of Sartre: love is an illusion, because as soon as people meet, there is a desire for domination, and the eating up of one liberty by another. The reality of love is individuals striving against the powers of death and corruption by trying to use each other to have a feeling of life.

It is true that people who have been hurt quickly rebuild barriers and seek more to be admired than to be loved. They become frightened of love, for in loving we necessarily become vulnerable. We can be wounded if the person we love does not respond as we want, if our call for union is not answered as we would like it to be. A lover in some ways offers himself, without a barrier, in the moment of love, and if this offering is rejected, or scorned, then he suffers more deeply than anyone. A child abandoned by his parents, a mother by her child, a lover by a lover — these are people with wounds so deep that they may never be healed.

Love is also frightening because it means risk. It means respect for the liberty of the other person, and that means not being able to forecast how he will evolve. I can be faithful until death, but the other may not. And I too might be unfaithful for I sense my weaknesses. This is the risk of love.

We are also frightened of love because it is linked to a world of sexuality and procreation, which is at the same time beautiful and disturbing. It is beautiful because the existence of each person in this vast family of mankind, all through time and into the future, has come from the union of two people freely consenting to love one another. It is true there is rape; it is true that there are caricatures of love; it is true that there is infidelity. But it is rare that at the moment of conception there is no love, and this is the beauty.

Yet it is also disturbing, because we might wish that this union of love between two people could be less linked to the physical reality of procreation. We can talk about ways of preventing conception, or of abortion, but there is something violent in not allowing the fulfilment of what is implied. The physical and the spiritual are so closely intertwined in love that we are frightened. It is a mystery too deep for intellectual understanding and not easily resolved by law.

Yet there is beauty in the physical consequence of love, for it brings us back to the human condition, back to fidelity in time. Love is not simply an experience which opens us to the infinite; it is also a bond, a link which brings us into time. It is the marriage between time and eternity and its beauty is finally the reality of fidelity, of mutual affection and of lasting commitment one to another.

Love is an enigma and so it is frightening. We see how quickly love can become impure. Even the love of a mother for her child — which has always been symbolized as the purest of love — can become an expression of the mother's need to hold on to the child and prevent him from growing to freedom. We see in relationships between men and women how quickly jealousy can arise, how quickly the poetry, the kindness and the sensitivity can become a fear of losing the other, a lack of confidence which denies liberty. Love is not just a gift of myself, not just communion. It implies also a fear that I may in some way lose my consciousness of self if I am not loved.

So we discover that even in the most simple and apparently pure forms of love there are seeds which are ugly and selfish.

And yet, mankind at all times and in all ages is questing, thirsting, yearning for this perfect love. We are all yearning to find the perfect friend, the lover who will carry me, as I in some mysterious way will carry him, in our quest for the eternal, flowering in time.

Jesus comes to us under various names. Jesus is the healer, He is the shepherd who guides us. He is also the lamb, the sacrificed one who takes away the sins of the world. Jesus is the saviour, the teacher, the prophet. He is the Christ, son of the living God. He is the Son of Man.

But he has a secret name, and this is the name of the lover, and this is the fundamental person and being of Jesus. He is almighty, for He is our God. He commands over life and death. He commands the elements of nature and He can turn water into wine. But this power is not at the service of admiration; Jesus flees when men want to make Him king. Jesus is a lover; this is His secret which can hardly be proclaimed, for it cannot be known outside of an experience.

John the Baptist proclaimed Jesus as the Lamb of God, but he also proclaimed him as the spouse, as the lover.

Now a discussion arose between John's disciples and a Jew over purifying. And they came to John, and said to him, "Rabbi, he who was with you beyond the Jordan, to

128

whom you bore witness, here he is, baptising, and all are going to him." John answered, "No one can receive anything except what is given him from heaven. You yourselves bear me witness, that I said, I am not the Christ, but I have been sent before him. He who has the bride is the bridegroom; the friend of the bridegroom, who stands and hears him, rejoices greatly at the bridegroom's voice; therefore this joy of mine is now full. He must increase, but I must decrease."

John 3, 25-30

Jesus calls himself the spouse.

Then the disciples of John came to him, saying, "Why do we and the Pharisees fast, but your disciples do not fast?" And Jesus said to them, "Can the wedding guests mourn as long as the bridegroom is with them? The days will come, when the bridegroom is taken away from them, and then they will fast."

Matthew 9, 14-15

Jesus the lover calls forth the infinite in our hearts. He calls forth those deep energies of love which are hidden in our beings. And when He sends us the Spirit, it is the Spirit which awakens in us this call to love and to be loved. This is why the Spirit is the most gentle, the most quiet and the most tender of beings. He touches us in the very depths, where we are frightened and vulnerable.

My beloved speaks and says to me: Arise my love, my fair one, and come away.

Song of Songs 2, 10

God did not want, with man, the relationship of an all

powerful one to a creature. He did not just want the relationship of a father to a child, in the human sense of the term. He wanted the relationship with us that He has with His only beloved Son, who is equal to Him in all things.

> "Fear not, for I have redeemed you; I have called you by name, you are mine. When you pass through the waters, I will be with you .... Because you are precious in my eyes, and honoured, and I love you."
>
> Isaiah 43, 1, 2, 4

God calls us in some ways to be His equals, to be so united in Jesus that we become like God Himself, participating in his divine nature. This is the Alliance, the New Covenant. Jesus lives in and through the love of the Father and it is this love of the Father that He pours into our hearts by the gift of his Spirit. It is this love that transforms us and opens us up and calls us forth as lovers.

This is essentially the experience of prayer. When Jesus says, "I give you my peace, I leave you my peace," he is giving us the treasure of God which is the kiss of God. It is the resting of the beloved in the beloved. It is this experience of union with God which touches us in our very depths and which is already the calling forth to the infinite.

Jesus, the spouse, invites us to the wedding feast. And he tells us that the Kingdom of God is like the wedding feast of the son of a king, who invited many to come.

> The kingdom of heaven may be compared to a king who gave a marriage feast for his son, and he sent his servants to call those who were invited to the marriage feast; but they would not come. Again he sent other servants, saying, "Tell those who are invited, Behold, I have made ready my dinner, my oxen and my fat calves are

130

> killed, and everything is ready; come to the
> marriage feast."

But they were all too busy with their business. The king
was angry and sent his troops to destroy them.

> Then he said to his servants, "The wedding
> is ready, but those who were invited were
> not worthy. Go therefore to the thorough-
> fares, and invite to the marriage feast as
> many as you can find."
>
> Matthew 22, 2-4, 8-9

And Saint Luke even adds:

> Then the master said to his servant, "Go out
> quickly to the streets and lanes of the city,
> and bring in the poor and maimed and blind
> and lame."
>
> Luke 14, 21

Will we be among the invited, or among the poor who
hear his calling? Jesus calls to us, "Come."

This is the fulfilment of the whole of scripture. It is the
fulfilment of the secret movement of scripture, the
discovery that God loves mankind as a lover.

> Fear not, for you will not be ashamed; be
> not confounded, for you will not be put to
> shame; for you will forget the shame of your
> youth, and the reproach of your widowhood
> you will remember no more. For your
> Maker is your husband, the Lord of hosts is
> his name; and the Holy One of Israel is your
> Redeemer, the God of the whole earth he is
> called. For the Lord has called you like a
> wife forsaken and grieved in spirit, like a

wife of youth when she is cast off, says your God. For a brief moment I forsook you, but with great compassion I will gather you. In overflowing wrath for a moment I hid my face from you, but with everlasting love I will have compassion on you, says the Lord, Your Redeemer.

Isaiah 54, 4-8

Therefore behold, I will allure her, and bring her into the wilderness, and speak tenderly to her. And there I will give her her vineyards, and make the Valley of Achor a door of hope. And there she shall answer as in the days of her youth, as at the time when she came out of the land of Egypt.

And in that day, says the Lord, you will call me "My husband," and no longer will you call me "My Baal". For I will remove the name of the Baals from her mouth, and they shall be mentioned by name no more. And I will make for you a covenant on that day with the beasts of the field, the birds of the air, and the creeping things of the ground; and I will abolish the bow, the sword, and war from the land; and I will make you lie down in safety. And I will betroth you to me for ever; I will betroth you to me in righteousness and in justice, in steadfast love and in mercy. I will betroth you to me in faithfulness; and you shall know the Lord.

Hosea 2, 14-20

This relationship of love, which is sung in the Song of Songs, symbolises this union between the heart of man and the heart of God. To those who have experienced God, truly and deeply, He reveals Himself as the lover, whether they are Christian or Hindu or Moslem. This is true of St. John of the Cross, Teresa of Avila and the great mystics of all time. God is the one my heart loves and who communicates to me in some mysterious way a deep interior warmth, a fire, a flowing of living water. He communicates to me a thirst, a desire, an overwhelming peace, for God communicates and gives Himself to man in the very depths of his being. When He touches me, He opens me, and at the same time He gives me a thirst to die, for this experience of God is only a taste of the eternal wedding feast. We are called in this afterlife not just to a knowledge of God, but to total union with Him as the lover, as the beloved.

> **Alleluia: For the Lord our God the Almighty reigns. Let us rejoice and exult and give him his glory, for the marriage of the Lamb has come, and his Bride has made herself ready; it was granted her to be clothed with fine linen, bright and pure.**
> **Revelation 19, 6-8**

While on earth, there will be moments of love when the Spirit calls me forth in the depths of my being to taste the Spirit in peace and to rest and abide in love. This is a prefiguration of the eternal wedding feast. It is the beginning of eternal life, to know and rest in the Father.

> **And this is eternal life, that they know thee the only true God, and Jesus Christ whom thou hast sent.**
> **John 17, 3**

These fleeting moments of love which can certainly inspire and orient all our lives will flower out in totality when we meet the Father face to face. Kiss to kiss. There in the life to come, after our bodies have died and especially when they are risen, we will explode into the wedding feast, we will enter the eternal celebration.

133

> Then I saw a new heaven and a new earth;
> for the first heaven and the first earth had
> passed away, and the sea was no more. And
> I saw the holy city, new Jerusalem, coming
> down out of heaven from God, prepared as a
> bride adorned for her husband; and I heard
> a loud voice from the throne saying,
> "Behold, the dwelling of God is with men.
> He will dwell with them, and they shall be
> his people, and God himself will be with
> them; he will wipe away every tear from
> their eyes, and death shall be no more,
> neither shall there be mourning nor crying
> nor pain any more, for the former things
> have passed away."
>
> Revelation 21, 1-4

But on earth we must continue as pilgrims of hope, sometimes walking in the night. That is why our constant cry must be, "Come." And that is why also the whole of scripture ends with:

> The Spirit and the Bride say, "Come." And
> let him who hears say, "Come." And let him
> who is thirsty come, let him who desires
> take the water of life without price.
>
> Revelation 22, 17

Jesus calls us all to live this experience of love in some way. But some are called to live it more deeply. For this is in reality the experience of the alliance and the covenant. Our God is a lover. So it is normal that Jesus will call forth some to virginity and to celibacy, so that they might offer themselves totally in all their being to the touch and the hope of the alliance. Those who answer His call to celibacy are, in some way, a special sign of the uniqueness of this love of God. Though of course, those who are married can and do have this experience of love.

Celibacy is particularly difficult in a world like ours which does not believe the message of Jesus and which knows less about the communion and fidelity of love than it does about sexuality, a world which can mock at love through television and cinema. This is why it is important that Christian communities come forth where people can live celibacy, not as a burden, but as a sign and a taste of that promise through long moments of prayer and rest with the spouse.

We are not above all called for activity. Our life is not just for the transformation of this world, for if it was, we would be in a never-ending circle. If we want to transform this world, it is so that all may become lovers. That is why before transforming the world we must ourselves become lovers and open ourselves to the experience of love, the experience of the infinite which is very fragile and begins in the quiet murmurings of peace. It is here, in some moments of prayer, or after receiving the body and the blood of Jesus, that we sense the first calls of the Spirit to the wedding feast, to a meeting with the spouse, to the marriage of the lamb.

If we are faithful to these first callings, the call will become deeper, the experience more living. As we cut ourselves away from those things which hold us back from the spouse, we enter into the state of fidelity which we must continually live if we wish to enter more deeply into the world of communion. The communion with Jesus in peace is the sign that we are already partaking in the reality of the wedding feast.

The Spirit and the spouse call "Come."

And Jesus says, "Bring in everyone to the wedding feast."

11

The Gift of Today

Jesus calls us forth to his patience and his impatience. He helps us gradually to accept people as they are, without judgment or condemnation, with all their defects, difficulties and bitterness, and their hopes, ambitions and capacities. He helps us to look at the other person and to understand him, and when this understanding has been born, perhaps to help him grow according to the music of his being, giving him the nourishment he needs. This is patience — to accept reality as it is; to accept ourselves with all our poverty, our weaknesses and our wounds.

There are a lot of people who weep when it rains and then find the sun too hot when it comes out. In winter they long for summer, in summer for autumn. Small people pretend to be big, and old people dress themselves up to look young. We always want to appear other than we are, instead of discovering the beauty of youth and of age as they come.

We should learn to rejoice in the gift that is today. Even if we fall sick, we should rejoice; for there's no point in fighting it, and it's a good time for quiet reading and prayer. We should relax in sickness and relax in health, accepting both as gifts from the Spirit.

So many of us live either in the past or in the future. Young people think it will be wonderful when they get out of school; but it isn't, for they enter the world of work. So they say it will be wonderful when they marry; and **so it** may be, for the first weeks, until the frustrations creep in. So they say it will be wonderful once the babies arrive; but then there is screaming in the night. So they look to the time when the children grow up, and how wonderful it will be to be alone. But when the children do grow up, they hang onto them. And then finally they get old and start to reminisce about how wonderful it was in the old days, when they were young. This is how we can pass through life without living.

One of the best qualities of the men and women I live with is that they live for the present. They have sufferings in their past and they have aspirations for the future, but because they are people whose hearts are more developed than their minds, they have the capacity to live in the reality of the present.

We have had some wonderful pilgrimages together. Once in Portugal, our bus started billowing smoke from the wheels. This seemed a bit odd, so we limped into a town and as we didn't have money for hotels, we went and knocked on the door of the priest. We trooped into his office and sat down, and when he came in and saw our motley crew his eyes popped out of his head. We were just singing and praying, completely abandoned to what might happen. I asked if he could find us somewhere to stay for the night and although I think he was quite keen to get rid of us, he was very kind. He put us in a big dormitory but didn't manage to find us any dinner. So there we were, about fifteen of us, in this hot room, with about three plums and a bit of stale bread each, and some tepid water. We asked each of our men what they wanted to drink, and when they said orangeade, that's what they got — even though it was really only the tepid water. So we had everything you can think of — champagne, burgundy, lemonade. It was really beautiful, the way each person lived the reality of the tepid water!

On the way back, I was driving the bus when suddenly

there was a great explosion — the windshield had shattered. I couldn't see a thing, but was trying to avoid a car I'd seen coming the other way before the bang and keep out of the ditch at the same time. In the middle of all this, Dédé said, "Isn't it beautiful! The windshield looks just like crystal." That's living in the present moment; that's seeing the beauty of reality!

In all things, wherever we may be, we must learn to welcome the reality and the people the moment brings us. If ever the central heating breaks down, if ever a man comes to mend a lock in your home, be vigilant: he might not be the best at his job, but he might be sent by God to hear the message. This happened once in Paris, when a locksmith and a friend of mine spent hours talking about Jesus. He was a person just as the barber you go to is a person. These are the people we are living with at this particular moment; these are the ones God has sent for a meeting. This is the now, and this is where we must learn to live.

Certainly we must plan, we also have "appointments in Jericho." But when the future becomes the now we must learn to be able to modify our plans in the light of the new information we have, in the light of the present needs of the people involved. We must be prepared to change our plans and to listen to the call of the moment. Wisdom begins when we stop wanting to fight the reality of the present as if it should not exist, and start to accept it as it is.

Our hearts must be filled with hope and they must be impatient, but our hope and our impatience must be based on the reality of the now. It is in this reality of the moment that Jesus will speak to us, that the Spirit will give Himself to us. We have to learn that God loves us, that we are precious to Him, and that we can abandon ourselves to His Spirit in the present moment.

Therefore do not be anxious about tomorrow, for tomorrow will be anxious for itself. Let the day's own trouble be

sufficient for the day.

Matthew 6, 34

The Spirit will give us tomorrow what He wants us to live tomorrow, but we must not waste time worrying about it. We should live the beauties of the relationship we have with Jesus and His Spirit and with each other in the now. We must become like children living in wonderment and in trust. The Spirit will give us the peace, the strength and the love to live tomorrow when it comes. Now, He gives us the strength to live this moment. That is why we must rejoice at all times, rejoice in what he is giving us now — the joys, the sufferings, the peace, the hopes. This is his gift to us today.

It is only when we learn not to fear, but to trust in God's love, to surrender ourselves, that we learn to relax. God likes relaxed children. He doesn't want us to strive to be perfect. He wants us to be confident that He will give us strength.

There are times of presence and times of absence in our life of love with the Spirit. There are times when we sense the Spirit of God in us, when we sense a love for the enemy, a death of aggressiveness, a flowing of the peace which is unity among people. And there are times when we are confused, when everything seems hard. At these times we tend to weep and say that God has forgotten us. We forget that the life of love is like the seasons — that there is spring and there is the harshness of winter. We forget that winter is important too, that nature needs to sleep, that frost is necessary for the rebirth of spring. There is the season of rain and the dry season; each complements the other.

We must go through winters of suffering, through times when prayer is hard and people no longer attract us, but spring is not far away. A death in the family, a failure in work, a sickness which brings a new way of life, an unfaithful friend, all these are wounds to the heart which take us into a period of darkness. This darkness is important. We must learn to be strong and peaceful in darkness, not fighting it, but waiting. We must learn to accept this winter as a gift from God, and we will discover that the snow will melt and the flowers come up.

> **We know that in everything God works for good with those who love him, who are called according to his purpose.**
> **Romans 8, 28**

This is how things of the Spirit are — a linking of time and eternity, with moments of communion and moments of fidelity. There are the spring times which are moments of communion and peace and rejoicing in the Spirit. And there are times of fidelity when we are close to Jesus, He who agonised more than any of us, and we say, "Let this cup pass from me; nevertheless, not as I will, but as thou wilt." (Matthew 25, 39)

We have to be very careful in times of winter not to be seduced by compensations. We may spend too much time in useless leisure or unending talk because of our solitude and our anguish. If we are celibate, we may dream that things would be better if we were married. If we live in a large community, we may dream that life would be happier in a small apartment. Some of our dreams may be true. But we have to be careful of winter dreams.

We must learn to live through the winter, for it is a profound part of any relationship. No community of people is really born until it has worked through tension and aggression. It is when we have worked through these — whether we are a community, husband and wife, or collaborators in work — that we find each other in a new way.

So it is with the Spirit of Jesus. His first call is a call of peace and quietness, and we go forth with great rejoicing. But then He wants us to grow strong in our love and our faith. He wants us to grow in a love which is never shaken.

> Who shall separate us from the love of
> Christ? Shall tribulation, or distress, or
> persecution, or famine, or nakedness, or
> peril, or sword? As it is written, "For thy
> sake we are being killed all the day long; we
> are regarded as sheep to be slaughtered."
>
> No, in all these things we are more than
> conquerors through him who loved us. For I
> am sure that neither death, nor life, nor
> angels, nor principalities, nor things
> present, nor things to come, nor powers,
> nor height, nor depth, nor anything else in
> all creation, will be able to separate us from
> the love of God in Christ Jesus our Lord.
>
> **Romans 8, 35-39**

To be able to say this, we have to go through the
strengthening times, which are the times of winter. We
have to discover gradually the anguish at the heart of the
universe, to discover the role of sacrifice, the role of
suffering, the role of the offering.

I think of a woman in Montreal who has been immobile
for fifteen years and is pretty well in constant pain. Yet it is
she who carries, in great part, any retreats and meetings I
might have. She never leaves the presence of Jesus; she
cares, in her crucified body, and she knows how to sustain
people. She has transformed her suffering, by a gift of the
Spirit, into a gift of Love.

Some people enter into the paths of sacrifice, love and
offering not just for their own fulfilment and growth, but
for the giving of life. They are offering up the wounds of
their being so that they may be close to the wounded ones
of the universe, so that the love which flowed from the
crucified Jesus might not be wasted but bears the fruit that
it should.

There are people in our world so wounded, so hurt, with defences so great, that it is impossible to speak with them. They reject immediately and violently any gesture which speaks of love; they cannot even be approached.

Who will meet them? It is not those followers of Jesus who are themselves deeply wounded, or close to despair. It is those who live in agony, but live this agony in the quiet light of God, praying for those who are in agony outside this light, for those who are in despair and committing various forms of suicide. It is those who offer themselves in sacrifice who can be close to the suffering ones of the universe.

This is why old age is important. It is a time of quiet contemplation, a time of offering. It can be a life of unchanging prayer, resting in the presence of God, accepting the wounds of fatigue and age and perhaps rejection and humiliation, for the wounded of the world.

We must learn to enter into and discover the meaning of the cross of Jesus. We must discover the meaning of sacrifice and of the closeness of death to resurrection, of suffering to joy. We must discover the mystery of the Lamb of God who takes away the sins of the world — the one who accepts suffering to take away the violence that has come from the exploitation, the lack of understanding, the indifference of those who have power and riches. This can only be done by those who enter the quiet domain of sacrifice.

I think of a young sister who offered her life for the black people of America. She had come to a big city to see her parents, and was sleeping in the spare room of a little fraternity. A young member of a gang, who knew the fraternity well, shot a revolver into the sky in the middle of the night. The bullet came through the window, ricocheted and went into the heart of the girl. This is to me a deep mystery of love; for many years she had wanted to give her life for justice for the black people; a mystery that she should have been killed by a revolver shot by a friend of the community, who did not know until much later that she had offered up her life for his people.

There is a mystery of suffering and of reparation at the heart of the universe. The exploitations, the wounds, and the sufferings of so many people who are shut up in hospitals, in prisons and in ghettos, who are despairing and lonely, who are hungry and thirsty, cannot be cured in a day or simply by a smile. They demand something much deeper; a reparation of suffering, even to death.

We have to enter into a deeper understanding of the sufferings that Jesus gives us. We have to discover that they can be a source of life for wounded people. We have to say, "Not my will, but yours, that humanity may find some peace and strength through this mystery that you are calling me to live."

For this sacrifice is also part of our very being. All of us are called to death. This is our reality, the message of our being, and at a given time it will become the message of the present moment. We can either accept or flee the different forms of death of our being. Fleeing them we seek compensations, or we accept and welcome them as a gift and an offering to our Father for the suffering of humanity and the sins of the world. We can offer and give our separations, our wounds, our mental and physical sufferings to God and thus enter into the mystery of the Lamb of God.

If we enter into this message of death, it can quickly become the message of life. We can assume death as a gift, as the gift which brings us finally to the wedding feast, to the total transformation of our being into love.

It will be there, in a special way, that we will discover the presence of the Silent One, of the woman of compassion, who stood for three hours beside her dying son, who was present in every fibre of her being to her crucified Jesus. She was inside Him by all the power of her love and compassion, by all the power of peace that was in her. Those who have been wounded or have experienced agony very quickly discover the role of compassion. A young adolescent can perhaps ignore this need for compassion, as he tends to ignore the mystery of death, of suffering, this mystery which is fundamental to our universe. When we are in anguish, when we are close to despair, we realize how much we need the presence of Mary, for she gives us a deeper understanding of the Cross, she helps us to live crucifixion and death. With her, bringing us nearer to Jesus, a new hope is born.

Our universe is a wounded universe, divided, suffering, with great despair and poverty, where there are many signs of death, division and hatred. But all of these signs of death are taken up in the Cross of Jesus and transfigured in the Resurrection. Our hope is that the winter of humanity will gradually be transformed to the bursting forth of love, for it is to this that we are called.

We will pass through the winter of suffering to the kingdom of God and rebirth. We can begin to sense them already, as the peace of the Spirit comes into our hearts, quelling bitterness and recreating hope. We sense the light which is a tiny sign of what we are called to live in the glory of the wedding feast of eternity.

As yet, we have to walk the paths of life. As yet, we are pilgrims walking towards the kingdom and the promised land with our brothers and sisters, through our wounds and those of humanity.

But we can say with hope, with confidence, with trust, "Come, Come Lord Jesus."

And he will answer, "Yes, I am coming soon. Yes, I am coming for you who are yearning for love. Be not afraid to love."

Come, Lord Jesus, Come.